GARDENERS' WORLD

BOOK OF

BULBS

GARDENERS' WORLD

BOOK OF

BULBS

SUE PHILLIPS

BBC BOOKS

PICTURE CREDITS

A–Z BOTANICAL COLLECTION page 75 (top); ARCAID page 10, 34 (top), 62, 78; BRUCE COLEMAN page 7 (top right and centre) 15, 27 (bottom), 39 (top left), 50, 66 (top), 67, 79 (bottom), 86 (top), 94 (top right), 99; FLOWER COUNCIL OF HOLLAND page 51 (left); THE GARDEN PICTURE LIBRARY page 3, 18 (bottom), 19 (top left and right), 23 (bottom), 46, 58, 59 (top left), 70 (bottom), 82, 91 (bottom left), 95 (right), 98 (bottom left); SUSAN GRIGGS AGENCY page 7 (top left and bottom right), 26, 30, 54; IMPACT PHOTOS page 23 (top right), 66 (bottom); INTERNATIONAL BLOEMBOLLEN CENTRUM Courtesy of Bulb Information Desk, page 11, 14, 18 (top), 19 (bottom), 23 (top left), 31, 38, 55, 71 (right), 74 (bottom), 86 (bottom), 91 (bottom right), 94 (top left), 95 (left); SUE PHILLIPS page 27 (top left and right), 59 (top right), 79 (top); PHOTOS HORTICULTURAL page 34 (bottom left), 98 (bottom right); HARRY SMITH HORTICULTURAL COLLECTION page 7 (bottom left), 22, 34 (right), 35, 39 (top right and bottom), 42 (left and bottom), 47 (bottom), 51 (right), 59 (bottom right), 70 (top), 71 (left), 74 (top left and right), 75 (bottom), 83, 87, 90, 91 (top), 94 (bottom), 98 (top); SYNDICATION INTERNATIONAL page 59 (bottom); ELIZABETH WHITING AND ASSOCIATES page 43, 47 (top).

Published by BBC Books,
a division of BBC Enterprises Limited,
Woodlands, 80 Wood Lane, London W12 0TT

First published 1990
© Sue Phillips 1990

ISBN 0 563 36099 2

Set in Kennerley by Ace Filmsetting Ltd, Frome

Printed and bound in England by Clays Ltd, St Ives Plc
Colour separations by Dot Gradations Ltd, Chelmsford
Cover printed by Clays Ltd, St Ives Plc

CONTENTS

Introduction	**8**
1 Choosing and planting bulbs	**11**
Buying bulbs	11
Choosing bulbs that suit your growing conditions	12
Planting bulbs in the garden	13
Cultivation tips	16
2 Gardening with bulbs: spring	**31**
Design guidelines	31
Borders	33
Containers	40
Rockeries, raised beds and sink gardens	44
Wild and woodland gardens	48
Bulbs for naturalising in lawns	49
Cut flowers	52
House and conservatory	53
Greenhouse and cold frame	56

3 Gardening with bulbs: summer   63

Design guidelines   63

Borders   64

Containers   69

Rockeries, raised beds and sink gardens   72

Wild and woodland gardens   75

Cut flowers   76

House and conservatory   77

4 Gardening with bulbs: autumn/winter   83

Design guidelines   83

Borders   84

Containers   89

Rockeries, raised beds and sink gardens   92

Cut flowers   93

House and conservatory   93

Greenhouse and cold frame   97

Informative index of bulbs   102

Useful reference books   108

Mail order nurseries supplying plants mentioned in this book   108

Index   110

INTRODUCTION

Bulbs are probably our most underestimated garden plants, yet they have enormous potential, particularly for small gardens. They can be the centre of attention in their own right, or provide the finishing touch to many intriguing plant associations. And, depending on which bulbs you choose, they can be used to add seasonal colour, architectural shapes, fine foliage or interesting detail to any style of garden. The possibilities are endless.

In informal gardens, dwarf bulbs can be grown carpet-like in a lawn or underneath shrubs, and taller species can be grown in clumps among other flowers for a contrast in shape, or up through shrubs or roses for a 'cottagey' effect. In a 'designer' garden, the strong shapes and unusual colours of some bulbous flowers can contribute enormously to the unique atmosphere of, perhaps, a white garden. In formal gardens (which are now coming back into fashion), bulbs can be used to edge borders, fill in geometrically shaped blocks, or as dot plants, forming a centre-piece to an important bed. There are species suitable for a whole host of purposes: for wild or woodland gardens; for containers on a patio; naturalised in grass and on banks; for rockeries, alpine sinks and raised beds; and for cut flowers.

The purpose of this book is to try to show the various ways bulbs can be used creatively all round the garden; not only to make the most of them, but also to make more of the other plants growing with them. It also demonstrates how bulbs help to create a garden that has something of interest coming into flower all the year round, luring you out to discover what new surprise it has in store today.

WHAT IS A BULB?

The term 'bulb' is commonly used by gardeners to describe a whole group of plants that lay down reserves of starch in special storage organs. In the wild, these structures, which incidentally are not always underground (think of a cyclamen), are a useful means of enabling a plant to survive hot dry summers or cold winters. When conditions become too extreme, the plant simply sheds its leaves and stems and, when the weather improves, it grows a new set from growth buds held safely inside the storage organ. A dormant bulb is really a naturally pre-packed plant held in 'suspended animation' and waiting only for the right set of conditions to trigger it back into growth.

Botanists, with their penchant for accuracy, sub-divide plants that behave this way into bulbs, corms, tubers and rhizomes, according to the various minor anatomical differences between them. But to gardeners, whose chief interest lies in growing plants rather than classifying them, the general term 'bulb' is quite adequate. So, even if it isn't technically correct, that is what I have used throughout this book.

1

CHOOSING AND PLANTING BULBS

BUYING BULBS

Bulbs are usually sold 'dry', while they are dormant. During the late summer and autumn, you'll find spring-flowering bulbs such as daffodils and tulips on sale. Summer- and autumn-flowering bulbs like tuberous begonias, gladioli and lilies are available in spring. Garden centres stock a good range of the more popular bulbs, pre-packed in bags with colourful instructional labels, but increasingly you'll find some of the less common varieties sold this way too. Cheaper varieties for naturalising (i.e. planting randomly in small groups or carpets to give a natural appearance) are usually sold loose from 'bulk' boxes – just pick up a bag and help yourself.

But, however you buy your bulbs, take a good look at them first. Choose only those that are firm and healthy-looking, and avoid any with cuts, dents or diseased patches. Also, reject soft or shrivelled bulbs, and any which have sprouted long, yellowish shoots. Bulbs with short, thick, green growth buds appearing at the tip, however, are perfectly sound – they just need to be planted quickly. Prices vary according to the size of the bulbs. The biggest generally cost more but produce the most flowers. Small bulbs may not flower much, or even at all, in their first year, simply because they have not

A selection of healthy dormant bulbs ready for planting.

reached flowering size. But, if you don't mind waiting a year while they grow, they can be an economical way of stocking a garden on a budget.

If you want to see a bigger range of varieties, especially the more unusual ones, then send for the mail order catalogues of the big bulb companies. These are very well illustrated and often contain a lot of helpful advice on things like height, flowering times and any special requirements of individual varieties. There are also several small companies specialising in choice bulbs (usually very desirable but often harder to grow) for enthusiasts; they generally produce printed lists only. Addresses for small and large bulb companies are listed at the back of this book.

Bulbs can be ordered quite confidently by mail order. They travel well in the dormant state, and since the bulb companies do most of their business by post, they are naturally concerned about keeping their customers happy. I've bought bulbs by mail order for years and never been disappointed with them yet.

Always try to buy bulbs when you will be free to plant them straight away. If you can't for any reason, then open the bags so the bulbs can 'breathe', and keep them somewhere cool (but frost-free) and out of direct sunlight.

A very few species can be tricky to establish if you buy them as dry bulbs. Snowdrops are one; these have a very short dormant season and some dry bulbs may, in fact, be dead. If you can, buy snowdrops 'in the green': as clumps of foliage, in spring, after the flowers are over. Hardy cyclamen are a similar case. Here, dry corms can be very difficult to get re-rooted, so again it is best to buy growing plants in pots.

You also sometimes see spring bulbs sold as growing plants in tubs or large pots, ready to take home. This is a good, if rather expensive, way of making sure you don't miss out on your spring display if you forget to buy dry bulbs at the right time. First make sure they are well hardened off if they have been growing under cover, then simply 'plunge' the pots into gaps in the border or stand them on a patio. After flowering, they can, of course, be planted out in the garden in the same way as bulbs grown in pots indoors.

One last thing to check when buying bulb species is that they have been grown in Britain, not collected from the wild. (It is only the species, not the cultivated hybrids, that are at risk here.) If in doubt, ask the supplier to confirm their origin. You'll be doing your bit to help plant conservation.

CHOOSING BULBS THAT SUIT YOUR GROWING CONDITIONS

The ideal soil for bulbs is one that is well-drained but contains plenty of organic material. This isn't quite as contradictory as it sounds; it simply means that the bulbs have access to moisture but are never waterlogged. Most popular bulbs will grow happily in a wide range of soils and situations, but some are much fussier. So, before buying, it is a good idea to check the conditions in your garden. Find out if the soil is neutral, slightly acid or alkaline by using one of the cheap soil-testing kits available from garden centres. And know your soil type by squeezing a handful of moist soil to see if it is clay (holds together in a ball) or light and sandy (feels gritty and shatters if you try to form it into a shape). Somewhere between the two extremes lies a good loamy soil, which is usually darkish in colour and can just about be formed into a rough ball, though it falls apart easily.

It is also a good idea to make a mental note or, better still, a sketch plan of the garden, so you know which beds are always shady, which are in full sun, which receive direct sun for about half the day, and which are in light dappled shade cast by trees or tall shrubs. You can, of course, alter the prevailing conditions to some extent (for instance, by making a raised bed for plants that like drier conditions), but this is a relatively major undertaking. It is normally much simpler to grow any plants that don't like the garden soil in pots filled with a suitable compost.

PLANTING BULBS IN THE GARDEN

Little soil preparation is needed for bulbs if the soil has previously been well cultivated. If it has not, spread a layer of well-rotted organic material, such as peat, garden compost or old manure, 2–3 in (5–7.5 cm) deep over the ground to be planted and add a handful of bone meal per square yard (or a special bulb fertiliser as instructed) and dig it in. On heavy soils, add one or two bucketfuls of grit per square yard as well to improve soil aeration and drainage. Dig that in too, mixing it well with the soil.

Then, lay the bulbs out in roughly the position you want to plant them, perhaps in straight rows as an edging to a formal bed, or more informally, in groups of threes and fives. If you are naturalising bulbs in a bed or lawn, just scatter them over the ground and plant them where they fall.

A hand-trowel is the best thing for planting bulbs, provided you only have a few to put in. If you have a lot of planting to do, it is easier to use a special bulb-planting tool: this consists of a handle with a hollow metal tube at the end. When pushed into the soil, it removes a core of soil leaving a hole that the bulb can simply be dropped into.

The important thing when planting bulbs is to make sure they are planted at the right depth. As a general rule, bulbs should be planted at approximately twice their own depth. This means that a bulb measuring

Bulbs vary enormously in shape and size according to the species. Lily bulbs may be as big as your fist, while some of the smaller bulbs are no bigger than a fingertip. Not all bulbs have a recognisable top – those of some anemones, for instance, e.g. 'De Caen', look more like three-dimensional pieces of a jigsaw puzzle. (With these there is no right way up.)

Naturalised bulbs make a superb show in a lawn, provided you plant a dense carpet.

2 in (5 cm) from base to tip should be covered with 4 in (10 cm) of soil. Make the hole slightly wider than the broadest part of the bulb and drop it in, taking care it lands the right way up. Firm the bulb gently into position with a light press and twist. This makes sure the base is in good contact with the soil: essential for good root formation. Then fill the hole with good soil, or a mixture of soil and peat or compost. There are always the odd special cases that need slightly different treatment. Some species need specially deep or specially shallow planting, so check in the reference pages at the back of this book. On heavy soil, it is a good idea to place a handful of grit at the bottom of each planting hole for drainage. And, when planting crown imperials, lay the bulbs on their sides to prevent water settling in the large hollows in the top, as this can lead to rotting. Finally, after planting a group of bulbs in a border, be sure to mark the spot with a label. Otherwise it is all too easy to cut into them with a hoe, or stick a fork through them when trying to plant something else on the same spot, which is most exasperating.

When naturalising bulbs in the lawn, the easiest way to plant them is to strip the turf from the area before improving the soil and planting as suggested above, then replacing the turf. Or, if this is not practical, use a trowel or bulb planter to remove a circle of turf for each bulb. Then make the planting hole a bit deeper than usual to leave room for a handful of soil/peat mixture. Plant the bulb into that, fill the hole with more of the same mixure and replace the divot.

CULTIVATION TIPS
BULBS NATURALISED IN BORDERS

Wherever bulbs are naturalised, they can usually be left undisturbed for many years. They will, however, benefit from occasional feeding; the same regime that suits the rest of the border will be perfectly acceptable to the bulbs. Apply a general-purpose feed, such as fish, blood and bone meal or Growmore, in April. (Where bulbs are growing with roses, use rose feed instead.) Repeat this about six or eight weeks later, and finally add a dressing of bone meal or superphosphate in early autumn. In time, naturalised bulbs produce offsets and can build up such overcrowded colonies that they no longer flower well. If this happens, dig up the clumps and divide them after the foliage has died down. Otherwise leave them alone.

One common problem people find with bulbs is that after the flowers are over, the foliage can make borders look very untidy. It is not a good idea to tie the leaves into knots or cut them down, as this prevents them feeding the bulbs which in turn means fewer flowers next year. Instead, leave the foliage to die down naturally. Borders can be made to look tidier if you plant spring bulbs towards the back, so their leaves are hidden by plants that grow up in front of them later. Or, instead of growing large hybrid daffodils and tulips which produce a lot of foliage, try dwarf narcissi instead; they have much smaller leaves which are less noticeable. It may also help to grow early varieties like 'February Gold', as they die down a bit sooner than later-flowering kinds. As for dead-heading, it's entirely up to you whether you dead-head or not. It is often recommended and, if you have the time and patience, it certainly won't do any harm. However, bulbs that are thriving can quite safely be left with their seed-heads on. And, if you grow the species, you may find it is a good idea to do so, as they shed seed which, given good conditions, will grow and gradually form bigger colonies than via natural increase by offsets. (Bulbs will increase naturally by forming offsets round parent bulbs but you will obtain a faster rate of increase from seeds, although new plants will be slower to start flowering than offsets.)

BULBS NATURALISED IN LAWNS

Rather than scattering bulbs about all over the place, many people like to plant them in drifts or on a bank. This not only looks better but also makes the area much easier to manage because, when the flowers are finished, the grass should not be cut until after the bulb foliage has died down naturally, otherwise the following year's flowering will be spoilt.

Like bulbs in borders, those naturalised in a lawn need feeding. But again, the same routine you give the lawn is ideal for bulbs. Feed the entire lawn, bulbs too, with a spring and summer lawn feed in April. (Don't use one which includes a selective weedkiller as this will distort or kill bulbs.) This feed can be repeated six or eight weeks later. Follow up with an autumn lawn feed in late summer or early autumn. Like bulbs naturalised in borders, those in lawns are best left undisturbed unless they become overcrowded and flowering suffers, in which case they can be dug up and divided.

WILD AND WOODLAND GARDENS

Contrary to popular belief, these are not just gardens that are left to run wild, but are carefully cultivated to enhance the natural landscape. In these types of garden, it is not normally recommended to use fertilisers, as wild flowers (other than bulbs) grow better without them. Chemicals should be avoided so that there is no risk to wildlife. However, if you are growing bulbs in woodlands, it depends very much on which ones you grow as to how best to cultivate them. Genuinely native wild bulbs such as wood sorrel and bluebells can grow perfectly well without feed or any attention other than the removal of brambles and so on. However, lilies are popular bulbs for lightly shaded woodland or natural-style borders and these do benefit from special care. In spring, lilies should be given a mulch of thoroughly composted

Left: Large, late-flowering hybrid daffodils leave a lot of unsightly floppy foliage after the flowers are over. You can avoid this problem by growing miniature daffodils, especially early-flowering ones like 'February Gold' which have smaller leaves that die down earlier.

Right: If space is needed for other plants – perhaps summer bedding – then bulbs of many species such as these narcissi, can be lifted after flowering, when the foliage has died down. After drying thoroughly they can then be stored ready to replant at the usual time. This way you will be able to observe the natural rate of increase of the bulbs, which form small offsets around their bases. When nearly as big as the parent bulb, these can be detached and planted separately.

Top left: Bulb planting is much easier using a special bulb planter, which lifts out a 'core' of soil, leaving a hole the right shape and size.

Top right: Bluebells make a good carpet of colour in a woodland-style garden. Their foliage acts as good ground cover after the flowers are over, so cutting down on weeding.

Left: Snowdrops grow well in the shade under trees. You can either plant a complete carpet, group them roughly in drifts, or arrange clumps around features such as fallen logs or tree trunks.

organic material such as peat or garden compost. The young shoots also need protecting from slugs. If you do not like using slug pellets, there are alternative remedies such as a saucer of beer in which slugs will drown themselves, or a very old-fashioned remedy that still works – surrounding the shoots with a circle of weathered soot. Avoid hoeing or otherwise disturbing the soil too much in woodland gardens as some lilies, particularly the giant Himalayan lily (*Cardiocrinum giganteum*), will propagate themselves readily from seed. In shady or undisturbed beds, weeds will probably be much less of a nuisance than in normally cultivated garden beds, but a mulch of bark chippings or fallen leaves makes a nice natural weed smotherer.

BULBS USED AS BEDDING

Instead of being left permanently in place like naturalised bulbs, bedding bulbs only occupy the ground temporarily. They are planted in the same way as before, fed with a dressing of bone meal at planting time and a general-purpose fertiliser such as Growmore in spring. But, after flowering, when the ground is cleared to make way for summer bedding, the bulbs are dug up, even if their leaves are still green. They are then planted in a row in a spare piece of land until their foliage dies down naturally. When they are dormant, the bulbs are lifted and stored ready for replanting next season. Although this is an old traditional technique, it can still be very useful in formal gardens or where space is short, and, with certain modifications, it is the way almost all bulbs are grown in containers.

TENDER SUMMER BULBS

Tender bulbs, such as tuberous begonia, canna and tigridia, are often started in pots in a heated greenhouse or on a window sill indoors and stood out in the garden after the last frost, around the end of May. If you do not have the facilities, dry bulbs can be planted straight into the garden or outdoor containers around this time. They won't, however, start flowering as early. The bulbs will need liquid feeding regularly throughout their growing season, from about six weeks after the first foliage appears. After flowering, let the leaves die down naturally, dig the bulbs up and store them in a dry, frost-free place for the winter. If foliage is not completely dried out when there is a risk of early frost, bulbs can be lifted and allowed to finish drying out indoors before storing.

SPRING BULBS IN
CONTAINERS OUTDOORS

Bulbs like narcissi, hyacinths and tulips are often used as spring bedding in patio tubs and troughs. To get a really good show, plant two 'tiers' of bulbs in the same container. Half fill each pot with a good peat- or soil-based potting compost – don't use garden soil. It is possible to re-use the old compost in the container after the previous summer's bedding plants are removed. Space the bulbs close together, but not quite touching. Then cover them with an inch (2.5 cm) of compost and plant a second layer of bulbs over the first. Cover these with compost, burying them so the tips are just below the surface. Then water lightly. Keep the containers somewhere cool and shady, where they won't be standing in water or under a drip, while the bulbs take root. (On a sheltered patio, they can be left in their normal position.) Move the containers to their final position when flower buds start appearing. Water sparingly at first, but, when the buds show, start giving regular liquid feeds until the flowers are over and the foliage has died down. Then lift the bulbs, clean off any remaining compost and dry them thoroughly before storing.

ROCKERIES, RAISED BEDS AND SINK GARDENS

These all provide a specialised environment for choicer dwarf bulbs such as small fritillaries, tiny species narcissi and other special little bulbs that need sunny, well-drained, sheltered conditions. Pockets of leafy or peaty soil can also be made in shadier corners for hardy cyclamen. These sorts of bulbs are all naturalised permanently in place, along with small alpine and rock plants.

When preparing a rockery, raised bed or sink garden, start with a base of good, coarse drainage material. Broken bricks and rubble can be used under a rockery or raised bed, while a layer of broken crocks or coarse gravel is ideal for the bottom 2 inches (5 cm) of a sink garden. A mixture of loamy topsoil and grit is good for raised beds and rockeries; for a sink garden use a mixture of 50% John Innes No. 2 potting compost and 50% potting grit. Decorate with large stones of your choice. Nowadays, the traditional idea of a rockery, where you try to duplicate the natural rock strata, has rather fallen from favour as, unless very well made and on a large scale, it tends to look very artificial. Scree gardens, or raised beds where stones are just used for decoration rather than to form the main structure of the bed, are much more popular and practical. Whichever way you choose to grow your rock plants, after planting cover the surface with a thin layer of stone chippings: these improve surface drainage and look attractive.

Rockeries and raised beds need little aftercare part from weeding, although this needs doing often to prevent small plants being overwhelmed by rampant weeds and smothered. Look out, though, for plant seedlings which should be left or transplanted elsewhere; a lot of dwarf bulbs seed themselves freely given suitable conditions. Unfortunately, a lot of choicer alpine plants and dwarf bulbs are very prone to rotting and, if you grow them on the rockery, they need protecting with a sheet of glass or a

Lilies such as 'Black Magic' associate specially well with old-fashioned roses and herbaceous plants. They prefer a situation where their tops are in sun but their bulbs and roots are shaded by surrounding foliage. Most lilies are happiest in lime-free soil. If your soil isn't neutral or slightly acid, they can be grown in large pots of lime-free potting compost, grit and loam and then sunk into place in the garden.

Right: Carefully chosen bulbs in containers can make a striking combination.

Below: Dwarf bulbs such as *Iris reticulata* are good for growing on a rock garden.

Above: Tender summer-flowering bulbs like tuberous begonias must be kept in a heated greenhouse or indoors until after the last frost.

cloche in winter. Sink gardens need more attention. In winter, keep the soil on the dry side and protect delicate plants from excess rain. In summer, regular watering will be necessary in dry spells. Feeding is not needed – the compost should supply all that is needed. But, every three or four years, turn out the sink and replace the compost entirely, dividing any plants that need it at the same time.

OUTDOOR BULBS INDOORS

Compact, spring-flowering outdoor bulbs such as hyacinths, dwarf narcissi, crocuses and snowdrops are most suitable for indoor use. You can use ordinary bulbs, the same as you would buy to plant in the garden, or those that have been specially prepared for early flowering. Both are treated in the same way, but, whereas ordinary bulbs can be planted at any time in the autumn, the specially prepared ones must be planted as soon as they are available – late August or early September – if you want them to flower in time for Christmas. Plant the bulbs in pots or bowls with or without drainage holes. Half fill the container with potting compost or bulb fibre, spacing the bulbs close together but not quite touching. Press each bulb firmly down into the compost and then cover them with more compost, leaving just the tips showing above the surface. Water enough to moisten the compost without leaving it soggy. Then place the containers somewhere cool and out of direct sun, per-

haps on a shelf in the garage, or plunged in soil in a shaded cold frame. You can even bury them under a few inches of peat at the foot of a north-facing wall. Cool conditions are essential to allow the bulbs to form roots. After about eight to twelve weeks, depending on the species, green shoots will start to appear. The pots of bulbs can now be moved under cover, but still need keeping cool and shady; a cold frame, greenhouse or glass-fronted porch is ideal. If you take them indoors, choose a very cool place, out of direct sun. Begin liquid feeding regularly and water them enough to keep the compost just moist all the time. Don't move the bowls into a warm room until the flower buds have appeared and are sufficiently developed to show their true colour, or the flowers may never open. Even so, the cooler you can keep them, the longer the flowers will last. When the flowers are over, return the containers to a cool sheltered place outdoors to let the foliage die back naturally. Then plant the bulbs in the garden.

The only exception to this growing method is *Narcissus tazetta* – 'Soleil d'Or', 'Paper White' and 'Chinese Sacred Lily' being the best-known varieties. These are not hardy and should not be put in the garden at all. These fast-growing varieties are looked at in more detail on page 97.

INDOOR BULBS

Many tender species of bulbs are grown permanently indoors or in a conservatory as pot plants. The technique for growing indoor bulbs is not all that different from growing any other houseplant, except that most of those grown from bulbs will lose their leaves and become dormant for part of the year, during which time they should be kept dry. Tender bulbs are sometimes sold as growing plants, otherwise they are available as dry bulbs in spring or autumn. If you are starting with dry bulbs, plant one large bulb or a group of small ones in pots large enough to hold the bulbs with an inch (2.5 cm) or so of space round the edge. Most kinds need only to be barely covered, leaving the tips showing above the surface of the compost. Water lightly after planting, then keep the soil on the dry side until new shoots start to appear, then water slightly more often as growth speeds up. Start feeding with liquid houseplant feed from the time flower buds appear, and continue feeding regularly all the time the bulbs are in leaf. Most bulbs grown as houseplants follow the same sort of growth cycle as outdoor bulbs and gradually become dormant again after flowering. But some species, notably hippeastrum and vallota, may either go dormant or decide to keep growing all the year round. So, watch them carefully and respond to the plants' behaviour: if the leaves continue growing and remain green, carry on feeding and watering normally; if they start to yellow, reduce feeding and watering and allow the bulbs gradually to become dormant. While they are dormant,

most houseplant bulbs can be left in their pots with the compost kept dry. Tuberous begonias, however, are safer removed from their pots, cleaned of compost and stored in a paper bag in a cool, dry, dark place; they tend to rot otherwise. Wait until bulbs indicate that they are ready to start growing again by producing small green shoots. This is the time to re-pot them if they need it, and resume watering, lightly at first.

BULBS IN GREENHOUSES AND COLD FRAMES

Many different kinds of bulbs can be grown in a cold frame, a cold greenhouse, or one heated just enough to keep it frost-free. These tend to be the more specialist kinds: the choicer and more expensive hardy bulbs, such as new daffodil hybrids, alpine house bulbs, plants for exhibition, and any that need some protection from winter wind and rain. Under glass, they can be watched more easily then out in the open garden. Slightly tender species can also be cultivated in a frost-free greenhouse, or a cold frame heated with electric soil-warming cables, though bulbs needing to be kept at more than about 40°F (5°C) are most economically grown indoors or in a conservatory.

Given that such a wide range of specialist bulbs are cultivated under glass, it would be unwise to offer too much general advice on cultivation. Each species should be considered individually. However, the following points apply to all:

Above left and right: 'Special' small bulbs are often grown in pots and sunk in sand in a bulb frame or alpine house where they can be given individual care.

Above and left: Perfumed flowers are specially valuable in spring; both in the garden and indoors. Lily of the valley (*above*) and hyacinths (*left*) are both unmistakable.

1) *Watering*

In winter, care needs to be taken with watering, as many winter-growing species are very susceptible to rotting. Species that are dormant in winter should be kept absolutely dry. In summer, bulbs that are summer-growers need quite a lot of watering, while, conversely, winter-growers that are dormant should be kept virtually dry. Some bulbs need only be grown under cover for the winter and can have their pots plunged into soil in the garden or an open cold frame for the summer.

However, a lot of enthusiasts' bulbs are grown permanently under glass and, especially with these, it is often helpful to make up a sand bed (either on the staging or in the border) into which pots can be plunged up to their rims. To make a sand bed, cover the staging (preferably the solid rather than the slatted sort) or the border with a sheet of polythene, and make a low wall round the edge with timber or bricks to give a bed about 6 in (15 cm) deep. Fill with sand, which should be the gritty horticultural type, not building sand. By keeping the sand moist in summer and drier in winter, the compost in the plunged pots can be kept moist enough without needing too much individual watering. The sand also insulates the plants' roots from extremes of heat and cold, all of which makes it easier to grow them well.

2) *Ventilation*

Good ventilation is very important. Even in winter, the ventilators should be opened for a few hours whenever the weather allows. In summer, the glass covers of cold frames should be removed entirely. It is useful to have a light wooden frame covered with Rokelene (a woven plastic mesh), or similar shading fabric, to prevent plants scorching on hot days. In a greenhouse, extra ventilators in both the roof and sides of the house are useful, and automatic ventilator openers are essential unless you are always at home to open and close them by hand. (You don't need electricity laid on to the greenhouse to use automatic ventilator openers.) It is also helpful to be able to leave the door open for extra ventilation – a Rokelene-covered frame is useful here to keep cats and birds

out. In summer, it may help to shade the glass slightly, using one of the liquid shading products you spray on, which can be washed off again in autumn. Shading will keep the inside of the greenhouse a little cooler and cut down the need for such frequent watering. However, certain bulbs, particularly some of the collectors' favourites like choicer tulip species and winter-growing bulbs such as freesia, do need a warm, sunny summer to ripen them for next year's flowering, so don't overdo it.

GROWING BULBS FOR CUTTING

Some bulb flowers, such as gladioli, are likely to be needed in quantity for flower arranging, so the best plan with these is to grow them in rows in a separate cut-flower bed or in the vegetable plot. In this way, you can cut every single flower without spoiling the look of your ornamental garden. It is also much simpler to manage flowers properly when they are growing in rows, where they are cultivated more like a vegetable crop than a flower border.

Prepare the ground for planting in autumn by digging in very well-rotted compost or peat, and grit if needed to aerate heavy soil. Shortly before planting spring-flowering bulbs (in autumn), rake in a dressing of special bulb fertiliser or bone meal. For summer-flowering bulbs, which are planted in spring, rake in a dressing of general fertiliser, such as Growmore or blood, fish and bone, just before planting. Plant the bulbs in straight rows, spacing them a few inches apart and allowing a path wide enough to walk between rows. As the foliage appears, start hoeing regularly between rows to keep them clear of weeds, and tie the developing stems of tall or top-heavy flowers to canes to keep them straight and unbroken. Feed regularly with liquid feed from the time flower buds first appear.

The flowers can be cut as soon as the buds just begin to open. (Don't cut immature buds, particularly of spring-flowering bulbs, as they may not open at all.) After flowering, continue feeding the bulbs until the foliage dies down and then lift, clean and store them to replant the following season.

This improved cultivation should result in good-sized blooms that develop their full colour and have strong stems, ideal for cutting. But, if you don't have room to grow flowers for cutting this way, or for those varieties you need only in small quantities, you can often include them in the garden borders as usual. In this case, simply plant more than you normally would, to allow some for cutting. When you cut, either take flowers from the back of the group, or thin them out all over, rather than make a big gap anywhere, thus damaging the garden display. Feed the borders in spring, summer and autumn, as usual, but try to give the bulbs a few extra liquid feeds when they come into bud.

2

GARDENING WITH BULBS: SPRING

Spring bulbs and blossom are something to look forward to, so plant them together to make a worthwhile display that shows up from a distance. Don't worry too much about subtlety – there's time for that later when there is a bigger range of flowers to play with.

DESIGN GUIDELINES

At the end of a long winter, the first spring flowers – snowdrops, winter aconites, crocuses and early daffodils – are such a welcome sight that few people really bother much about how they fit into the design of the garden. The fact that they are there is what matters. It's not until later in the season, when the novelty of having lots of flowers around has worn off, that we start getting choosy about which plants look best grown together. But, lovely as those first spring flowers are, it is still important to make the most of their display potential. After all, you are unlikely to go outdoors much during cold weather, so the earliest spring flowers will mostly be seen from the house. This means either growing the flowers close to the house, or making the distant view an impressive one. Better still, why not do a bit of both?

The very earliest spring flowers are particularly small ones, so the place where winter aconites, snowdrops and crocuses will make most of an impression, especially if you only have a few of them, is close to the house, growing in containers or small beds by the front or back door, or on the patio outside the lounge windows. From a distance such small, light-coloured flowers don't make much of a 'show' if they are just dotted thinly around. So, to make a real impact, they need to be planted in large blocks, carpet-like, under trees or shrubs, or perhaps in the lawn. But that can be expensive; a similar impact can be created much more economically by 'arranging' spring bulb in groups in such a way that they form part of the structure of the landscape.

Different kinds of bulbs can be arranged with each other, or, more effective still, teamed with whatever else your garden has to offer of interest at the same time: other types of spring flowers, all-year-round plants like evergreens, conifers, shrubs with colourful bark, or architectural features like seats or tree stumps. In this way, it is easy to organise relatively little material into a series of attractive plant 'cameos' that are much more interesting to look at. There is no need to worry that some parts of the garden are left green; plain areas will make a perfectly natural-looking background to your spring features – in fact, a green background will accentuate your feature areas all the better. And, in a small garden, you'll find that trying to cram in too much spring colour leaves you seriously short of space in which to grow plants that flower later in the season. (This

is an important consideration when you think that most people plan their garden to look its very best in summer; spring and autumn, though still important, usually take second place.) So, avoid the temptation to try to fill the whole garden with spring bulbs. A few well-designed spring features look far better, and can be completely filled with a mixture of spring bulbs and other early-flowering plants, in the knowledge that, when they are over, other parts of the garden will become the centre of attention.

As spring moves on and the range of flowers and new foliage increases, your plant cameos can become more imaginative; you can afford to be bolder with your use of plants and particularly colours. Most spring flowers are either pink or yellow – two colours you might not choose to mix together under normal circumstances. But, in spring, flowers and colours in the garden are still something of a novelty after a long, stark winter, and the eye is so relieved to see them it tends not to worry too much about colour clashes. This isn't the time for too much subtlety. Instead, concentrate on creating interesting plant associations that will attract the attention and encourage you into the garden to discover what new flowers have come out since the last time. The secret is to arrange your spring features so that, as you reach one, you can see a tantalising glimpse of the next: round a bend in a path, peeping out from behind the corner of a wall, a gateway or clump of tall evergreens, always leading you on, right round the garden.

The key to creating successful plant associations lies in observing the different patterns, shapes, sizes, colours and textures of plants and flowers, and matching them together in much the same way as you do, almost subconsciously, when choosing soft furnishings or clothes that 'go' together. It becomes much easier with practice, but looking at other people's gardens and noticing the way they have teamed plants up is a great help when you first start. Of course, when you try out your own planting combination, it is essential to check that the plants you want to put together in fact flower at the same time, and will grow happily in the same kind of conditions. The key at the end of this book should help here.

BORDERS

When it comes to colour combinations, virtually anything goes, at least until our post-winter craving for flowers has been satisfied. But by choosing contrasting plant shapes and tasteful combinations of colour you can, if you wish, create some very interesting and rather less predictable spring effects.

BULBS WITH OTHER SPRING FLOWERS

Daffodils are very versatile and they look good planted with green flowers. You could have groups of very early cultivars (varieties arrived at in cultivation), such as 'February Gold' or 'Tête à Tête', planted amongst the green-flowered hellebores, *Helleborus corsicus* and *H. foetidus*. Or, choose later-flowering daffodils to go with euphorbia; in a sunny spot, *Euphorbia wulfenii* associates especially well with the large-flowered hybrid daffodils that bloom in late March and April. Even before the euphorbia is fully out in flower it makes an interesting combination with daffodils; the young flower shoots are curved over at the tip rather like baby bracken fronds, and slowly uncurl as they start to develop into the characteristic huge, lime-green heads. For something more spectacular still, add an unusual species of peony, *Paeonia mlokosewitschii*, which has enormous, chalice-shaped, lemon-yellow flowers, and perhaps a nice, big, stone urn, to make a riveting cameo for a sheltered border near the house.

For a more colourful combination, try planting groups of daffodils (perhaps one of the double-flowered kinds like 'Irene Copeland', or one of the flamboyant butterfly narcissi such as 'Love Call' or 'Tricolet') with a carpet of different coloured polyanthuses, including lots of bright reds and oranges, or mixed hyacinths, containing a good range of blues. Alternatively, plant traditional cultivars like 'King Alfred', or a mixture of naturalising kinds, with the big, yellow daisies of doronicum for a natural-looking cottage-style plant combination. For a sophisticated green and white corner,

Left: Spring 'corners' can be based round a colour scheme, or some feature of the garden. A darkly romantic woodland garden is lit up with pinpoints of white tulips.

Bottom left: A wilder type of garden, where patches of *Narcissus* 'February Gold' have been used to highlight a variegated holly surrounded by a carpet of variegated periwinkle, to form a golden border.

Below: For a less sophisticated look, choose a riotous mixture of colours – you can get away with anything in spring!

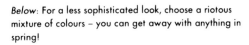

Opposite: Small groups of bulbs are welcome 'discoveries' on a walk around the garden. Tuck them in to odd corners by a seat or on a bend in the path.

a few groups of leucojum (snowflake) make a subtle combination planted with green-flowered hellebores and the upright tree ivy, *Hedera congesta*, in a carpet of the broad, marbled foliage of *Arum italicum* 'Pictum'.

BULBS WITH SHRUBS

All sorts of spring bulbs can be used very effectively in a mixed border of shrubs and flowers. Early-flowering viburnums and camellias are two shrubs that always look well together, and many of the early viburnums are beautifully scented, making up for this deficiency in the camellia. A few bulbs, however, will 'pull' the combination together even better. A lot of people like to play safe and plant white flowers, such as snowflakes, with pink flowers; these look especially good with varieties of camellia with pink and white streaked flowers. Add a ground-covering group of shocking pink *Primula rosea* to complete the scene.

The camellia/viburnum combination, however, looks even more interesting under-planted with a carpet of muscari (grape hyacinth). The soft, powder-blue colour and the texture created by the odd bunch-of-grape-like flowers creates a very pleasing picture. Add a few groups of pink daffodils like 'Passionale' or 'Waterperry', if you like, for eye-catching highlights. If you want to create something even more striking, group very bright pink or red camellias together with bright yellow or yellow and orange daffodils – it looks surprisingly good, and early spring is the season for getting away with combinations you might not want to chance at more flower-filled times.

For a quieter combination, try the blue winter-flowering iris, *Iris unguicularis*, planted with blue or grey conifers and purple or yellow crocus. The iris needs a sheltered south-facing spot and very good drainage to do well. Another attractive combination is a carpet of snowdrops or *Arum italicum* 'Pictum' with hellebores, at the foot of the evergreen *Garrya elliptica*, which is draped in long greeny-grey catkins in winter.

Particularly striking is the sight of a cream and green variegated shrub such as *Cornus alba* 'Elegantissima' with a mixture of daffodils. The opening foliage buds of the shrub make pinpoints of light among the large flowers which look most attractive. Another successful spring combination is daffodils followed a month later by tulips, planted with the brilliant orange spring foliage of *Spiraea × bumalda* 'Goldflame'. Daffodils, especially any cultivars with orange centres, also look spectacular planted with forsythia, especially if the shrub has a nice, large-leaved, deep-green evergreen such as rhododendron planted behind it to give some substance to the twiggy outline.

In a border filled mainly with shrubs, one very good way of adding a touch of spring is by under-planting reasonable-sized areas with low-growing bulbs like *Anemone blanda*, winter aconites, lily of the valley or snowdrops, all of which will grow happily in light shade. Unlike daffodils and other larger-growing bulbs, the foliage will not be a nuisance later – it is short enough not to look untidy. This ground-covering effect looks especially striking when you grow a multicoloured carpet of *Anemone blanda* in a shrub border: the brightly coloured, star-shaped flowers make a wonderful contrast with the bare twigs and evergreen foliage above them. Or, for something more sophisticated, team smaller carpets of single colour, such as winter aconite, with curiously shaped plants, like *Corylus avellana* 'Contorta' (contorted hazel), which has yellow catkins in spring, or with the sort of shrubs that are cut hard back annually to provide lots of coloured shoots for winter, like cornus, or some of the ornamental willows. A background of evergreen foliage, particularly a blue or grey shade, provides the finishing touch to an interesting grouping.

LATER SPRING BULBS

As spring moves on, a wider selection of bulbs will come into flower. The majority of large hybrid tulips will be out in May, and these associate particularly well with wallflowers. I especially like the combination of flamboyant parrot tulips (particularly the three-coloured ones such as 'Apricot Parrot', which is peach and orange, flamed with green, or a mixture such as 'Per-

sian Carpet' which contains a lot of red and marmalade orange colours) grown amongst dark red wallflowers. The elegantly waisted flowers of lily-flowered tulips seem most at home in slightly more formal surroundings, though they can look stunning grown wherever their shape makes a surprising contrast with other plant or architectural forms. Try the white 'White Triumphator', planted in informal groups amongst silver foliage plants such as artemisia, or with forget-me-nots. Or place a small group casually at the foot of a blue conifer, brick steps, or by the door of an old-fashioned brick-based greenhouse.

Green-streaked Viridiflora tulips look interesting grown amongst any kind of foliage, but particularly evergreens, so use them to add interest to groups of small conifers or small summer-flowering shrubs, like hebes, that have yet to start flowering. Their colour combinations are so extraordinary they do not need anything in the way of clever plant associations to make the most of them. 'Angel', for instance, has flowers striped in two shades of green and pale yellow, and it makes a sensational addition to a white garden. 'Florosa' is striped in green, chrome yellow and toothpaste pink – a small group is quite striking enough on its own without other colours around, but grow it with golden conifers to give them a lift.

Ordinary, large-flowered, hybrid tulips like the Darwin kinds are such formal flowers I always find them difficult to place

Anemone blanda makes a lovely carpet of colour under shrubs, especially under evergreens or those with coloured or contorted twigs.

Above: On their own, tulips look rather formal. You can soften the effect by blending them informally with wallflowers and old-fashioned double daisies.

Above: Particularly spectacular are the flamboyant Parrot tulips. These have extravagantly frilled petals often tinged with several colours. This is 'Apricot Parrot'; but eight or ten different cultivars are commonly available.

Left: Viridiflora tulips like 'Greenland' have equally spectacular flowers much valued by flower arrangers. Use them in the garden to add a touch of colour to a green and white border, or in groups as a contrast to large expanses of green foliage.

in informal borders; they actually look most at home in formal beds used as spring bedding. But there is no reason why you should not plant a few groups wherever you need a splash of May colour in a border: try to link them with other plants with interesting shapes like the bolt-upright flowering cherry, *Prunus* 'Amanogawa', or a vaguely mushroom-shaped amelanchier, and with leaf colours like the red of new peony foliage. Surprisingly, they also 'work' quite well planted in groups, in a well-drained, cottage-garden-style border, amongst carpets of border auriculas, *Primula auriculas*, whose colour range goes very well with tulips and provides an interesting contrast of shape as well.

Black tulips such as 'Queen of the Night' (which are really a very dark purple) associate very well with golden foliage, so try them with *Sambucus racemosa* 'Plumosa Aurea', the cut-leaved golden elder. The extravagant, frilly-flowered 'Black Parrot' looks better grown with plainer-shaped gold foliage, *Philadelphus coronarius* 'Aureus', for instance, or, less sophisticatedly, with the perennial wallflower, *Cheiranthus* 'Bowles' Mauve' (which used to be called *Erysimum*).

A particularly fascinating May-flowering bulb for growing in borders is *Fritillaria imperialis* (crown imperial). This has huge, solid-looking flowers of tawny orange on 2-foot (60-cm)-high stems. Crown imperials were once popular cottage-garden flowers, and used to be grown in formal rows in front of a wall, or standing out in groups from amongst a carpet of low-growing ground-cover plants. But they also look good planted informally to accentuate a nicely shaped group of medium-sized shrubs in a mixed border. The tawny orange shades of the flowers are nicely offset by honeysuckles and chaenomeles, both of which have the same cottage-garden feel about them. As well as the best-known orange crown imperial, there are also yellow and red cultivars and, rarer still, one with variegated leaves, and even one with 'hose in hose' flowers which looks as if one flower has been pushed inside another. These are just the thing where you want something a bit special. Another rather unusual member of the fritillary family, needing the same sort of conditions as crown imperials, is *Fritillaria persica* 'Adiyaman'. This produces lots of bell-shaped plum-purple flowers on 2 ft (60 cm) stems in May, and looks great growing amongst golden foliage, or pink, mauve and lilac flowers. It is not very well known, but deserves to be much more widely planted.

CONTAINERS

Containers of spring bulbs are particularly valuable in small gardens as they enable flowers to be grown in places where there is no soil; on paths and patios, for instance. They also enable flowers to be moved to wherever you will get most benefit from them, which, early in the year, will usually be somewhere close to the house. You can plant containers with all the same kind of bulbs, mix different kinds together, or even mix them with other early spring-flowering plants. But, to keep the display going for as long as possible, it is much better to grow each plant in a separate pot and then plunge them into a larger container filled with peat. In this way you can mix 'n' match whatever is in flower at the same time to best advantage and you can also easily remove pots whose flowers are starting to go over, and substitute new ones just coming into bloom.

Any of the smaller spring bulbs such as snowdrops, crocuses, miniature narcissi and grape hyacinths can be grown in your usual patio tubs and troughs, and even window boxes. But you need a few slightly taller plants – bulbs or otherwise – to add height. And, whether you have just one container by a back door, or a whole collection of planted containers arranged on a patio, you need a continuous factor linking them visually together. So, rather than have lots of different kinds of plants dotted about, try using one species predominantly as the main theme, with other plants adding minor variations.

HYACINTH THEMES

Hyacinths have to be your first choice if you want a powerful, fragrant scent, which makes them particularly valuable for containers near a front or back door. You can get different cultivars of hyacinths in blue, purple, mauve, red, pink or white, and even pale yellow, flowering at different times between late February and mid-April, so, by choosing carefully, you can have a continuous succession in flower over that period.

In small containers, you could plant hyacinths on their own, in one colour, for a formal display, or have several shades of one colour such as pink or purple and mauve, or plant a complete mixture of colours. In a larger container, you could add other bulbs too; this gives a more informal look which is rather attractive. Purple, blue or pale yellow hyacinths look nice planted with daffodils. Two shades of pink hyacinth, or pink and mauve, look good with blue muscari (grape hyacinths). Or, for a more natural look entirely, try adding one of the early-flowering water-lily-type tulips such as *Tulipa kaufmanniana* or *T. fosteriana* varieties, and perhaps some crocuses, to a container of hyacinths. The result is a lovely blend of shapes and colours, which softens the rather formal appearance that hyacinths can easily have on their own.

NARCISSI AND TULIP THEMES

Amongst the other bulbs that make good central subjects for a container planting scheme are narcissi and tulips; they are ideal for creating a more informal look. The smaller-growing hybrids of miniature narcissi, which are normally grown on rockeries, are preferable to the large-

Above: Bulbs do very well in tubs for a spring display. Here, double daffodils and hyacinths have been planted with *Cheiranthus* 'Bowles Mauve'.

Above: As well as all the better known bulbs, it is worth growing a few of the more unusual kinds. *Fritillaria persica* 'Adiyaman' always attracts attention but it does need the right background.

Right: *Tulipa kaufmanniana* are sometimes called water-lily tulips as their flowers open out flat. They are good for planting in containers as they don't have much foliage.

Smaller bulbs such as species tulips and grape hyacinth make a good combination for window boxes. When spring bulbs are over, they are replaced with summer bedding plants, leaving the ivy to provide permanent foliage.

flowered ones. (Large-flowered hybrids have lots of tall, untidy foliage that tends to flop unattractively over the sides of tubs.) For early flowering, 'February Gold', 'February Silver' or 'Tête à Tête' are all good choices that should flower late in February or early in March. For March flowering, try 'Jack Snipe' and 'Peeping Tom', and in April/May, 'Hawera', 'Thalia' or *N. triandrus alba*. Especially nice are the scented narcissi belonging to the Jonquilla group, such as 'Baby Moon', 'Lintie' and

'Trevithian', which all flower in April or May. Any of these will look superb mixed with polyanthus, coloured primroses or forget-me-nots, either in the same containers or in adjacent ones.

Tulips can also be grown in containers but, as with daffodils, the large-flowered hybrids can look untidy simply because they are tall and tend to flop when grown without the support of surrounding plants. Shorter-growing rockery-type tulips are much more suitable, especially the early-flowering *kaufmanniana* and *fosteriana* varieties which flower from the middle of March onwards. They make short, stocky plants, often only 6–8 in (15–20 cm) tall and in keeping with the proportions of most containers. The flowers of this type of tulip open out fully, giving them their popular name of water-lily tulips. Several cultivars have pale-petalled flowers with a striking circle of colour in the centre; 'Ancilla', for instance, is pale pink with a bright yellow central circle edged with red. They provide especially good opportunities for creating interesting plant associations; choose one of the minor colours from the tulip and add another flower of that colour – narcissi, for instance – to create an interesting co-ordinated look.

ROCKERIES, RAISED BEDS AND SINK GARDENS

In general, the sort of bulbs chosen for planting in rockeries and raised beds are the smaller kinds and those that prefer very well-drained conditions. Species and their immediate hybrids are usually preferred to the more flamboyant, large-flowered hybrids, as the former are more in keeping with the other kinds of plants that inhabit this rather specialist environment. Sink gardens are really just very small rock gardens in containers, whose proportions make them suitable for only the very smallest of rockery bulbs.

As regards design, here again, a few isolated plants dotted about on their own won't make much of an impact, so it pays to buy several of each kind of bulb and plant them in groups. In such a compact setting as a rock garden, I find the best plan is to create an all-year-round backcloth of evergreen plants which you then 'decorate' with seasonal highlights in the shape of flowers – bulbs in particular. Since rock plants, including many dwarf bulbs, are normally sold in pots while they are in flower, it's quite easy to test several different potential plant associations in the nursery before buying the plants. Any of the miniature narcissi and tulips suggested earlier for containers can also be grown on a rockery or raised bed. The difference is that in the rockery or raised bed they are more likely to be naturalised – planted permanently in place – than they are in containers, where they will almost certainly be treated as temporary bedding. Such flowers, large by rockery standards, associate well with robust, spreading plants like aubrieta, arabis and *Alyssum saxatile*.

For a less predictable effect, go for the smallest daffodil species, which can be planted in sink gardens as well as in raised beds or rockeries. These will encourage you to look closely into the miniature landscape that you can create. Particularly interesting species include: *N. asturiensis*, which grows only 3 in (8 cm) high and flowers in February with minute yellow trumpets; *N.*

bulbocodium, the hoop petticoat daffodil, growing 6 in (15 cm) high, which has flowers rather like yellow crinoline skirts; and *N. cyclamineus*, which has flowers that resemble a yellow Christmas cracker, with the outer petals swept back in the same way as a cyclamen, and flowers around February or March. Any of these tiny narcissi look best planted in small groups against a background of evergreens: interestingly shaped dwarf conifers such as *Chamaecyparis obtusa* 'Nana Gracilis', or the peculiar, spiky, upright *Thymus erectus*, perhaps, with a carpet of ground-hugging thymes like *T. serpyllum* or *T.s. minimus*.

Species tulips are another good candidate for rock gardens; they are small and neat, and particularly appreciate the warm, sunny summer rest, when bulbs are dormant, and well-drained conditions in winter provided by a rock garden. Again, the early-flowering ones are the most useful as there is so little else out in the garden then. These species also tend to be suitable for a rock garden as they are not as large and showy as the much bigger and later-flowering hybrids. *Tulipa pulchella* flowers in late March with pretty little pinky-violet flowers. Its variety, *T.p. violacea*, flowers earlier still, from February, and has similar flowers but shaded with purple and green. Both grow about 5 in (13cm) tall and are small enough for sink gardens. Another early tulip is the multi-headed bronze-and-white-flowered *T. turkestanica*, which also blooms in March.

This is larger, growing to 9 in (23 cm). *T. orphanidea* is a fascinating tulip, 8 in (20 cm) high but very much more delicate than *turkestanica*. Its flowers appear in April, tawny orange with olive streaks on the outside of the petals. *T. clusiana* (lady tulip) is perhaps more to everybody's taste; this has long, narrow, red-and-white-striped buds that are particularly elegant, on 10 in (25 cm) stems. Most eye-catching of all, though, must be the horned tulip, *T. acuminata*, which has extraordinary, long, narrow, flame-red and yellow petals quite unlike those of any other flower, let alone a tulip, that you have seen. This grows rather larger, to about 18 in (45 cm), so it needs siting carefully.

As a lot of tulip species have rather glaucous foliage, they associate nicely on a rockery with silvery foliage plants. The larger kinds look superb with *Hebe pimeleoides* 'Quicksilver', which has lots of tiny silver-blue leaves packed in a small, dense bush. Smaller and more delicate species look better with hillocks of *Artemisia schmidtiana* 'Nana' or *Convolvulus cneorum* (which may flower to coincide with the tulips with rather pretty, 1-inch (2.5-cm)-wide, off-white, typical convolvulus flowers). Add a different shape, such as tufts of the blue perennial dwarf grass, *Festuca glauca*, and you have quite a nice grouping. A scattering of *Hepatica nobilis* and groups of *Iris reticulata* will bring the same collection of evergreen foliage to life at the start of the

Above: An old stone sink makes a good place to grow plants that like well-drained conditions.

Above: Dwarf bulbs are also useful for bringing seasonal colour to a rock garden – here species of fritillary, narcissi, grape hyacinth and iris make an interesting display.

Opposite: A small, compact rock garden will provide an excellent environment for many dwarf bulbs which prefer well-drained conditions.

season, before the tulips. Hepatica has blue, star-like flowers, and the dwarf iris comes in various shades of light and dark blue; both flower in February and March. It is not important if any of these overlap with the tulips as they all 'go' quite well together. Or, if you like very unusual flowers, try growing some of the small fritillaries; these have nodding bell-shaped flowers usually in earthy shades of green, brown, terracotta or ochre yellow, or a combination of any of these colours, on slender grassy stems with fine lily-like foliage. They are not spectacular flowers, though fascinating to look at close up. They are also rather choice and sometimes difficult, so if they take your fancy it's worth experimenting with some of the cheaper and easier varieties first. Try *Fritillaria acmopetala*, which grows to about 15 in (38 cm) and has olive-and-purple-striped flowers in May, or *F. michailowsky*, which grows to about 6 in (15 cm) and has yellow-tipped mahogany-red bells in March/April, to start with. All need very well-drained, sunny conditions, and look best with a dark background, preferably away from brightly coloured flowers.

WILD AND WOODLAND GARDENS

Wild gardens are not just gardens left alone to grow wild, as some people think. They are cared for as much as other parts of the garden, but cultivated differently and using different plants. These may be genuine wild species, or cultivated plants that simply look more at home in natural surroundings than in a formal border. Often they are plants that need certain conditions most easily found in a wild or woodland garden: unfertilised soil, plenty of leaf mould, and light dappled shade. The more sun-loving species like lilies can be accommodated in small clearings.

If you have a small group of native trees in the garden already, it can be improved by the addition of bulbs and other flowers. Otherwise, it is surprising how easily the unique feeling of a natural planting scheme can be re-created in a small space by planting a few trees and shrubs, perhaps birch and pine with rhododendrons, or a collection of acers and evergreens. These act as the framework of the 'wood' with rough grass left between them, accented with bulbs and flowers. Grow some bulbs in carpets, others in groups round the bases of trees, and yet more in large drifts on their own, or in association with other shade-tolerant flowers or shrubs.

In spring, a carpet of bluebells uninterrupted by anything other than tree trunks is one of the true sights of natural woodlands. Unfortunately their foliage persists exceptionally late into the summer, so there is little else you can do with a bluebell wood afterwards. In a garden version, you can create a suggestion of bluebell woods by growing groups of bluebells amongst other plants; try them with rhododendrons, clumps of self-sown aquilegia and primroses.

N. pseudonarcissus (wild daffodils) or *Anemone nemorosa* (wood anemone) also make good carpets of colour in spring for lightly wooded areas. They blend well with violets, wood sorrel, celandine and wild strawberry. (Never dig up wild bulbs growing in a wood; cultivated bulbs of all the wild species are available cheaply, in quantities suitable for naturalising, from mail order catalogues.)

Other good carpeting plants for a lightly shaded woodland bed include snowdrops and winter aconites. Include a patch of spring-flowering hardy *Cyclamen coum* under a small tree, such as weeping birch, in leaf-mould-rich soil. To give a change of height to a small bed, add a colony of either the true wild daffodil or one of the species, near the bottom of a tree trunk. And in a special place, such as tucked into a niche by a fallen log, try using a small clump of erythroniums to form a focal point. The commonest one is *Erythronium dens-canis* (dog's tooth violet), which has pretty mottled leaves and pink flowers, but there are other varieties with yellow, yellow and white or mauvish flowers, which also look superb in this setting. The yellow-flowered kinds, such as *E. tuolumnense*, look especially interesting planted with a group of *Arum italicum* 'Pictum', whose cream and green variegated leaves accentuate the yellow of the erythronium flowers; in fact, they make better partners for them than the plants' own leaves do.

Another less common flower for wild and woodland gardens is *Fritillaria meleagris* (snake's head fritillary), a rare wild flower now commonly cultivated for sale in bulb form. This has large, nodding, bell-shaped flowers in purplish-mauve, marked with a distinctive chequered pattern. An all-white cultivar, 'Aphrodite', is also available and the two look good mixed together. Both kinds have slender stems 12–18 in (30–45 cm) tall, giving the impression that their flowers are hovering in thin air. Snake's head fritillaries will grow in sun or partial shade, but need moist soil and, given good conditions, they will seed themselves freely. In light shade, they look good growing with a low carpet of violets and celandines; in a sunnier spot, odd groups look good growing amongst paving or amongst hellebores or narcissi, while a really thriving colony looks best on its own, naturalised in grass round a wild pond.

BULBS FOR NATURALISING IN LAWNS

One of the nicest ways of growing bulbs in a natural-looking way, without establishing a separate wild or woodland area, is to plant them in drifts in the lawn. The sort of bulbs grown this way are those which can happily be left without needing frequent lifting and

Snake's head fritillary, *Fritillaria meleagris* is a versatile and easy-to-grow species, which is at home naturalised in moist grassland, wild gardens, or near a pond. It associates well with wild flowers, such as ladies' smock and wild daffodils, as well as more sophisticated flowers, and thrives in light shade under trees or perhaps in an old orchard.

Left: Bulbs make good cut flowers. In Holland they are used in all sorts of ways rarely seen in Britain.

Above: All sorts of bulbs can be naturalised in a lawn, but some of the nicest are the dwarf kinds like *Narcissus bulbocodium* and *Erythonium dens-canis*. Mixed together they recreate the look of an alpine meadow.

division but, most importantly, those kinds which are available cheaply in bulk. Mixtures of narcissi are sold specially for naturalising, but you can also use crocuses, grape hyacinths or snowdrops (good for a slightly shady spot). I've even seen waterlily tulips naturalised in well-drained lawns. Some people prefer to use specific types of daffodils for naturalising rather than mixtures, and one of the best is the old cottage-garden favourite, *Narcissus poeticus recurvus* (pheasant's eye daffodil). This is one of the last narcissi to flower and has a lovely scent; there is also a double form of it called *Narcissus poeticus* 'Flore Pleno'. However,

there is no reason why you shouldn't use any of the cheaper, large-flowered hybrid or species daffodils on their own, if you prefer.

In a lawn, bulbs can be naturalised to form a light carpet of bulbs evenly distributed through the grass, planted in informal areas under trees, or 'contour planted': grown in a shaped drift designed to add interest to a large expanse of lawn. They can also be planted in small groups in grass close to an existing feature, perhaps by a seat, or under a specimen tree or shrub, to add a touch of extra seasonal interest to it. One very nice informal cameo is a rustic seat made from a fallen log with a scattering of species daffodils naturalised beside it. The golden rule when naturalising bulbs in grass in any way is to keep it simple. Stick to one species (i.e. narcissi or tulips) for the main effect, perhaps using one or two others in small clumps as accents at the bottom of tree trunks.

It's not only level lawns that look good with bulbs naturalised in them. You can naturalise bulbs on a bank too; daffodils are the most commonly used for this purpose. In fact, this is one of the best ways of using a bank, as it not only makes it look more inter-esting, but also cuts down the amount of mowing you need to do – always more diffi-cult on a steep slope! If reducing mowing is your aim, I'd stick to large-flowered daffodil hybrids as they are taller-growing than most species and can be grown in quite long grass without getting lost. Add a few groups of primroses in shorter grass for a natural effect, particularly where the bank drops down into a damp ditch or stream.

CUT FLOWERS

Although most British gardeners have an in-built horror of cutting daffodils and tulips from the garden, spring bulbs do in fact make very good cut flowers. They are used a great deal on the Continent, especially in Holland, where a tremendous selection of varieties are readily available in flower shops, including unusual kinds and some we don't usually think of here as cut flowers,

like snowdrops and hyacinths. So, if you enjoy using flowers in the house, why not try growing a few of the sort you usually buy from the florist, as well as the more popular garden varieties? Favourite bulb flowers for cutting include anemones, Dutch iris, lily of the valley and 'Apeldoorn' tulips. Also try unusual-coloured flowers like the black and green widow iris, pink daffodils, or the green-streaked Viridiflora tulips, as well as the more interestingly shaped flowers like parrot and lily-flowered tulips, and double or butterfly daffodils.

HOW TO PROLONG THE LIFE OF ALL BULB FLOWERS

Virtually any bulb flower can be cut for arranging, with the exception of crocus. And though bulb flowers are reputed not to last long in water, they will if you treat them properly right from the moment you cut them. Here's the secret: take a bucket of tepid water into the garden with you and, as soon as you cut the flowers, stand them in water almost up to their necks. Leave them in a cool room out of direct sun for a few hours before arranging them. Then put a cut-flower feed in the water you use to fill the vase. If you can get the kind sold spe-cially for bulb flowers, use it even if you are arranging the bulbs with other kinds of flowers.

One or two bulb flowers have their own special problems. Daffodils are reputed to kill any other flowers you arrange them with.

This is due to the thick slimy sap that oozes out of the stems after they are cut. The solution is either to arrange daffodils in a vase on their own, or to cut the stems to the required length and leave them standing in a bucket of deep water for at least 12 hours before arranging them. Then, so long as you do not re-cut the stems, you can safely mix them with other kinds of flowers. The other problem flowers are tulips, whose stems tend to bend however you arrange them. Some people recommend sticking a pin through the stem just below the head of each flower – but this really is no help at all. Tulips should not bend if you cut them and stand them in water straight away; it's more likely to happen when they have been left out of water for some time. You can straighten bent tulips by rolling several stems in a small bunch together tightly in newspaper, and standing them in a deep bucket of water for several hours. But, no matter how well you prepare them, tulips will always turn towards the light. So rather than trying to force them into artificial shapes use them in informal arrangements where their natural movement won't matter.

HOUSE AND CONSERVATORY

Spring is probably the time of year when most bulbs are grown indoors. A large bowl of spring-flowering bulbs such as hyacinths or narcissi makes a good show on its own and is ideal for standing on a coffee table or sideboard. But you can create a much better display by plunging groups of individual pot-grown bulbs temporarily into a larger container while their flowers are at their best. You could, for instance, fill a large old-fashioned china washbasin to the brim with moss, and make a naturalistic arrangement in it using several pots of miniature narcissi and snowdrops, with pieces of corkscrew willow, driftwood, fir cones and similar flower-arranging accessories. Or use the same sort of idea to make a *pot-et-fleur* arrangement. Here, you use pot-grown flowering plants to provide temporary colour in an otherwise permanent arrangement of foliage plants. These again are best plunged, still in their pots, into any large ornamental container planted with foliage houseplants. Asparagus fern, foxtail fern (*Asparagus meyeri*), bird's nest fern, ladder fern, fatsia or ivy all make suitable foliage plants to accompany flowering bulbs. Tropical foliage plants are a bit too exotic-looking to team up well with them, though you could always experiment. For a more formal display, plunge a row of individually pot-grown hyacinths into a trough of moss or bark chippings (the sort sold for mulching the garden). This would be ideal for a window sill or perhaps a disused hearth.

FORCED LILY OF THE VALLEY

As well as all the usual spring bulbs, all of which have to be planted in autumn, you can force lily of the valley in spring. It doesn't take long, and a pot of flowering lily of the valley makes a lovely indoor plant; its scent is enough to fill a room. Just dig a few roots up from the garden in late February or early March, three-quarters fill a shallow, 5-in-(13-cm)-diameter pot with potting compost and lay the roots on top, with any buds you can see facing upwards. Cover the roots with about an inch (2.5 cm) more compost, water slightly, and leave on a not-too-warm window sill out of direct sun. Soon shoots will appear, and when the first flower buds start to open, you can stand the pot inside a pretty pot cover, and move it to a warmer spot anywhere in the house; the strong scent is a bit overpowering in a room where you'll be eating, though. After the flowers are over, replant the roots in the garden.

HOUSEPLANT BULBS

Besides spring bulbs that are only temporary indoor plants, the first of the permanent indoor bulbs will be starting to flower in spring. Hippeastrums can he expected to produce their huge and spectacular blooms any time from Christmas onwards. *Clivia miniata*, the Kaffir lily, should flower around April. And in March, a most unusual flower called lachenalia or Cape cowslip produces its remarkable flowers, which look rather like bluebells in shape, but instead of being blue, they are bright yellow, tipped with

Left: The Kaffir lily, *Clivia miniata*, makes an attractive houseplant. Its striking shape is shown off best by a plain background, with a colour-coordinated pot cover. After flowering, clivia can be stood out in a greenhouse, sunroom or enclosed porch, or used to provide the foliage interest to a group of summer-flowering houseplants.

Opposite: *Oxalis adenophylla* is an attractive bulb species for a sunny sink garden or rockery, though it is seen at its best grown in a cold frame or greenhouse with a collection of other 'special' small bulbs.

orange. The plants form dense clumps, and a good potful will be covered with flowers. Lachenalia flowers only last well if you keep the plant cool; they are best kept in the greenhouse and just brought indoors while actually in flower. Since both clivia and lachenalia are rather imposing, they are seen at their best grown as specimen plants in a nice but plain china or brass pot cover, and stood on a coffee table or sideboard where they have an uncluttered background.

Hippeastrums are the very opposite; on their own they are difficult to place attractively as they are such top-heavy-looking flowers, appearing at the top of a tall stem usually without any foliage to act as visual balance. I find they look much better stood in the centre of a group of foliage plants: asparagus, foxtail fern, fatsia, fatshedera and ivy look good with them, but, being that much more exotic, they could also be teamed with tropical foliage such as maranta. Foliage plants will take the bare look off the stem and give the flowers a bit of background. Otherwise, if you are really stuck for a novel display idea for a hippeastrum, why not consider cutting the flower to use as the centrepiece of an arrangement? It's done a lot in Holland.

One last bulb to grow indoors is a real curiosity, *Sauromatum venosum*. It is often sold under the name of voodoo lily and can be grown simply by standing the dry bulb in a saucer. It makes a fascinating 'pet' for children, and little boys, particularly, are likely to appreciate the extraordinary lurid flower, which appears on its own before any foliage grows. A single bud grows from the top of the bulb, which rapidly elongates into a 1-ft- (30-cm) -high maroon spike, and eventually unravels itself to reveal a grotesque maroon and yellow creation shaped a bit like an arum lily. The flower fortunately lasts only a day, as the smell is quite nauseating. But, when it is over, the bulb is worth potting up and growing on for its most attractive tropical-looking foliage, which makes a good foil for summer-flowering plants.

GREENHOUSE AND COLD FRAME

A huge selection of bulbs can be grown in an unheated greenhouse or deep cold frame. Any of the normal outdoor bulbs can be planted in pots and flowered in a greenhouse instead of being taken into the house. There is also a fascinating selection of choicer bulbs, both hardy and slightly tender, which are normally grown under glass.

CHOICE SMALL BULBS IN POTS

A lot of alpine-plant enthusiasts include unusual small pot-grown bulbs in their collections, and an amazing selection of varieties are available from specialist nurseries. Species cyclamen are very collectable: *Cyclamen coum* has pink flowers throughout winter and early spring, and its silver-leaved forms are especially attractive.

C. trochopteranthum has strongly scented purply-pink flowers with oddly twisted petals like a ship's propeller. And, in a frost-free greenhouse, you can also grow the slightly tender cyclamen species such as *C. persicum* (the wild parent of the modern florists' cyclamen) and *C. libanoticum*, which has prettily marbled leaves. *Oxalis versicolor* is a rather unusual plant that produces white flowers edged in red, which look very much like wood anemones. The buds are produced throughout the winter and spring. In dull weather they remain rolled up and look like old-fashioned peppermint sticks: white spirals with red stripes. When the sun comes out, the flowers open fully, making a complete cover over the delicate foliage. The better-known *Oxalis adenophylla* and miniature irises like *I. reticulata*, *I. histrioides* and *I. danfordiae* make nice plants for growing in pots under cover too. A lot of people also like to grow the tinier species narcissi such as *N. cyclamineus*, *N. rupicola* and the scented *N. jonquilla*, as well as the frailer species tulips like *Tulipa orphanidea*, under cover.

Pots of small bulbs look best, as well as being easiest to look after properly, plunged into deep trays of damp sand, leaving just the rims showing above the surface. (A special kind of greenhouse staging with deep sand trays is sold for growing alpines.) To make pots of flowering bulbs into an attractive display, arrange them with pots of dwarf conifers and evergreen alpine plants with interesting shapes and colours, such as silvery mounds of encrusted saxifrages, or coloured carpets of mossy saxifrages like the lime-green 'Flowers of Sulphur' and golden 'Cloth of Gold', or sempervivums (houseleeks). You can see this sort of display done very successfully in the alpine house at the Royal Horticultural Society's garden at Wisley in Surrey; when the flowers are over, pots are replaced with new ones from the cold frames outside. At home, if you don't have both a greenhouse and a cold frame, you can simply grow the same set of plants permanently under one or the other throughout the winter and spring.

GROWING PLEIONES

If you fancy trying something a bit more challenging, how about pleiones? These are small terrestrial orchids that grow only a few inches high, but have large and beautiful flowers in April or May. Pleiones are sold as dry bulbs during the winter and early spring. They should be potted as soon as you receive them, using a special compost made by mixing one-third each of fine orchid compost or chopped live sphagnum moss, John Innes seed compost, and grit. (If you buy from a specialist nursery you may also be able to buy pleione compost ready mixed.) To make a good show, get at least three bulbs of a kind. Use a small pot, only slightly bigger than the bulbs it is to house, and three-quarters fill it with the mixture. Stand the bulbs round the edges of the pot, not

Iris reticulata are a popular group of small bulbs ideal for growing in pots in a cold greenhouse for spring decoration. They can be brought into the house and kept in a cool room while the flowers are at their best. A wide range of varieties are available mainly in shades of blue and mauve. This is 'Harmony'. They all need gritty, well-drained compost. Don't overwater.

Pleione orchids are surprisingly easy to grow provided you give them the conditions they need. Though individual plants are small, a group makes a lovely display.

In a greenhouse, small bulbs are easier to look after if their pots are plunged in moist sand to the rims.

Fritillary species are very collectable, and many choice kinds, such as this *F. latifolia nobilis*, are available from specialist nurseries. Grow them under cold glass.

Freesias are slightly challenging to grow, but well worth the trouble as it is so rewarding when you cut your own crop of flowers. Fresh picked, they last as long in water as they would on the plant, and the scent is delicious.

quite touching, and place enough compost round them to hold them upright – don't bury them. Place the pot in a lightly shaded spot in a frost-free greenhouse. Keep the bulbs entirely dry until early March, when the pot can be given a very light spray with plain water on fine days. This is enough to start the bulbs growing. Pleiones will flower before producing their leaves, with comparatively large and showy blooms, for such small bulbs, in shades of pink and mauve. After the flowers go over, the leaves slowly start to grow and the plants need more water as growth speeds up. Keep them in a humid atmosphere and keep the compost just moist throughout the summer: the safest way is to stand the pot on damp capillary matting until the leaves start to die down. Then gradually reduce watering until the bulbs become dormant for the winter.

GROWING FREESIAS

Freesias are very popular as cut flowers, but the only way you can grow them for yourself is in a frost-free greenhouse; they don't do well indoors. So-called outdoor freesias are sometimes available but these have been specially prepared and can only be grown once. Freesias can be raised from seed sown in spring, potted into 3½-in (9-cm) pots and grown on in the greenhouse for the summer. They may flower that autumn or the next spring. After flowering, they will go dormant during the summer, and from then on should be treated the same as for freesias bought as bulbs. Plant bulbs in November in individual 3½-in (9-cm) pots using John Innes No. 2 compost mixed with a little extra grit for drainage. Leave the tips of the bulbs showing above the surface of the compost. Water the bulbs lightly in, and then stand the pots down on the border soil, sinking the bottom inch (2.5 cm) of each into the ground to keep them upright. From then on, spray occasionally with water, but do not water properly until the first green shoots start to appear at the tips of the bulbs. Then water very lightly and only when the compost is completely dry, until the roots have grown through the bottom of the pots and out into the border soil. (Lift a pot occasionally to check.) When the roots have grown through, only water the border soil, not the pots, whenever it gets dry. Add liquid feed occasionally, when the plants are making good growth. Then, when the flower buds appear, stop watering and feeding, and tie each stem to a split cane to keep it straight. Freesia flowers are ready to cut as soon as the first bud on each stem begins to open. After the flowers have been cut, resume feeding and watering the plants as before, but when the foliage starts to yellow, gradually reduce both until the bulbs become dormant. Then knock them out of their pots, clean and store them for replanting next autumn.

COLLECTORS' BULBS

Amongst the pages of the catalogues, you'll find several very special bulbs indeed: new hybrids, rare species, or antique varieties, particularly of tulips. These are invariably in short supply and therefore much more expensive than everyday varieties. So, although in theory they should be perfectly all right grown out in the garden, few people want to run the risk – they may be attacked by insects, eaten by voles, rot, or be accidentally cut with a hoe. Instead, it is normal to grow them in pots under cover where you can keep an eye on them. If and when you have built up your stock to a safe level, either by saving seed of species, or removing offsets from named varieties, you could perhaps try a few in the garden. In the meantime, you can make the most of your 'treasures' by bringing the pots into the house or conservatory to enjoy them while the flowers are at their best. Or, you could bed the pots out into a carefully chosen safe place in a border outdoors when the first shoots appear above the top of the pots, until after flowering. But avoid moving pots outside if the weather is very cold or windy, or waiting until the flowers are well developed: the sudden change of conditions could scorch the buds and spoil the flowers.

3

GARDENING WITH BULBS: SUMMER

DESIGN GUIDELINES

After the rush of brightly coloured spring bulbs that steal the scene at the start of the year, the summer-flowering kind follow on at a more leisurely pace, without making such a forceful impact on the garden. Summer-flowering bulbs have a different role to play, since they are most often seen against a background filled with flowers which they cannot always rival for colour. Instead, it is the geometrical shapes of their flowers and foliage that catch the eye: the large trumpet shapes of lilies, the neat spikes of liatris and the nodding umbrella-shaped clusters or precise spheres of ornamental onions are commonly found. To make the most of summer bulbs, they should be grouped with plants that emphasise their contrasting shapes and textures. In this way, what at first glance appears to be a large mass of colour can be broken down into a series of interesting plant associations which attract the onlooker to investigate more closely.

With so many different kinds of summer flowers – bulbs and otherwise – to choose from, it can be difficult to know where to start in deciding how best to combine them together. The way most people do this is by deciding on some sort of a theme for their planting: the look of an old-fashioned cottage garden; a traditional mixed shrub and herbaceous border surrounding a lawn; a semi-tropical patio; or a modern designer-style garden, perhaps with a specific colour theme. And, since most bulbs have well-defined flowering times, you can then choose and plant them to fill seasonal gaps in your overall summer display all round the garden – even growing a few in pots to stand in place when an odd gap appears that needs something to fill it. And, however flower-filled the garden may be, it is always nice to include a few unusual plants that have people asking, 'What's that?' Less well-known but striking bulbs, like dierama, acidanthera and tigridia, are a useful way of creating eye-catching points of interest in key parts of the garden. There are also many fascinating and unusual bulbs suitable for creating colourful displays in containers on patios, in the conservatory and indoors.

Wherever you choose to position bulbs, you'll find their strong shapes and bold characters play a useful part in creating the style of garden you prefer.

BORDERS

Groups of bulbs strategically placed in a mixed border make a striking contrast in shape and texture to the surrounding herbaceous flowers and shrubs. By adapting the type of plants you associate bulbs with, you can subtly suggest particular styles of garden ranging from the most modern to the traditional.

SPECTACULAR SHAPES - ORNAMENTAL ONIONS AND LILIES

One of the most useful families of bulb for flower shape are the alliums (ornamental onions), most of which flower in June and July. They include some with very strongly spherical shapes like the tall *Allium giganteum* which grows to 4 ft (1.2 m), *A. albopilosum* (syn. *christophii*) which is 2 ft (60 cm) tall but has flowers up to 4 in (10 cm) across, and *A. karataviense* which is only 12 in (30 cm) high but has the largest heads of the lot. All have rosy-purple flowers, but those of *albopilosum* and

karataviense have a noticeably metallic glint to them. If you group any of these alongside other plants with strong shapes, such as red-leaved *Phormium tenax* (New Zealand flax) and *Cotinus coggygria* (a shrub with disc-shaped reddish-purple leaves), you can create a distinctly modern effect. But team them with mauve-tinted old-fashioned roses, pink stocks and purple sage, and you have a romantic cottage-garden look. If you have a white garden, you'll find that the interestingly shaped, mauvish highlights of *A. albopilosum* or *karataviense* help to pick out the detail.

A. bulgaricum (*Nectaroscordum siculum* ssp. *bulgaricum*) is a useful plant for adding interesting shapes to a large colourful border. Its tall, pale cream, umbrella-shaped flowers stand out above the tops of most herbaceous plants and small shrubs, making a most imposing sight. At Beth Chatto's garden near Colchester, several groups of this plant are dotted between other plants in a large border, introducing a common theme that links the planting together most attractively. The same idea could be used in a small garden, in island beds, or borders of herbaceous plants, shrubs and conifers.

A. sphaerocephalum is another bulb that looks good grown in groups, this time in herbaceous and rose borders. It grows about 18 in (45 cm) tall and has smallish, bright mauve, oval-shaped flowers, which make stunning pinpoints of colour amongst pink, purple and cream flowers. A particularly good thing about *sphaerocephalum* is that, of all the alliums, it is one of the cheapest to buy and most widely available.

Lilies are equally versatile bulbs, which will pick up the flavour of whatever they are planted with. Traditionally hybrid lilies in a mixture of colours are grown in small groups amongst shrubs or old-fashioned roses in a big border. Here, their tall stately stems and wide-flaring flowers are a useful way of continuing the display in the border after the main flush of rose and shrub flowers are over. This sort of position suits lilies well; they grow best with their tops in sun and the bulbs well shaded by neighbouring plants. But, in a modern-style garden, try lilies in more ambitious associations: with bamboos and cut-leaved Japanese maples for an oriental look; or try white-flowered lilies, such as *Lilium regale*, with striking silvery shrub foliage, like the Prince-of-Wales-feather-shaped leaves of *Melianthus major*, which is a specially nice combination for a white garden. It also goes nicely with coyote willow, *Salix exigua* (which has long, narrow, silvery leaves), and other medium-sized silvery shrubs with architectural shapes or feathery foliage.

Another very widely grown lily is *Lilium candidum* (madonna lily). This is probably one of the oldest flowers in cultivation, and looks most at home in a cottage-garden setting surrounded by a tangle of other flowers. Unlike most lilies, this is not one that should be planted deeply – the tips of each bulb

should be left just showing above the soil surface. A very different shape again are the flowers of *L. martagon* (Turk's cap lily); these resemble a series of small pink or mauve Chinese lanterns hanging in the air. Again, grown amongst shrubs they make a delightful addition to contrastingly shaped foliage, or to a mixture of smaller massed flowers in either contrasting or toning colours. This, incidentally, is one of the least fussy lilies to grow, and thrives just about anywhere.

L. tigrinum (tiger lily) is another very popular species, with flaming-orange flowers heavily spotted with black. Like other bright orange flowers, it can be a little difficult to place in a lot of gardens, especially if their colour schemes are based on fashionable pastels or pink, mauve and purple. However, give the lily a background of evergreen foliage, such as the glossy *Choisya ternata* or rhododendron, or the matt *Viburnum rhytidophyllum*, and you'll see it at its most spectacular. Many lilies are scented, *L. regale*, *auratum* and *candidum* in particular, which makes them well worth including in planting schemes near a path or seating area in the garden.

OLD FAVOURITES

Moving on to the smaller families of summer-flowering bulbs, crocosmia (which used to be called montbretia) and hemerocallis are two very popular plants. Both are long established as traditional

favourites for herbaceous borders, and look their best grown in groups amongst a mass of other flowers of all colours. But, for a rather different way of using them, try placing them strategically in a garden based on different-shaped evergreens, conifers and grasses, to create seasonal spots of colour against a deep green background. Crocosmia grows about 18 in (45 cm) tall, with red or orange tubular flowers arranged in rows along the flower stem, and hemerocallis has

Left and below: In summer, the most outstanding feature of bulb flowers is their shape rather than their colour. The rounded heads of *Allium sphaerocephalum* (*left*) and the trumpet shapes of lilies (*below*) make a striking contrast with surrounding flowers and foliage.

Lilies are very versatile summer bulbs. The Turk's cap lily, *L. martagon*, grows well in partial shade which makes it ideal for naturalising under trees in a woodland garden, though it is also at home in a more formal shrubbery or mixed border. A white form of *L. martagon* is also occasionally available, which shows up better against a dark background. If you need lots of *L. martagon* to complete a scheme, plants can be grown from seeds, but expect them to take four to five years to flower.

a tighter cluster of lily-like flowers at the top of a taller stem 2–2½ ft (60–75 cm) high; these come in yellow, tawny orange, apricot and buff shades.

Gladiolus byzantinus is a smaller bulb you don't often see. It has vivid magenta flowers in early summer, and was traditionally grown as a cottage-garden plant. However, I think this rather underrated plant would be worth experimenting with using other types of plantings too. Try it, for instance, with the purply-tinted, feathery foliage of bronze fennel, or the stark upright shape of *Berberis thunbergii* 'Helmond Pillar', for a more modern effect. Unlike the better-known hybrid gladioli, whose bulbs have to be lifted and stored for the winter, *G. byzantinus* can be left out in the garden all year, and is in fact best left undisturbed to grow into large clumps.

UNUSUAL EXOTICS

One plant that will be sure to attract attention in late summer is *Acidanthera murielae*. This grows about 3 ft (90 cm) tall, and has gladiolus-like foliage but with large, sophisticated, white flowers, each having a purple 'butterfly' mark in the centre. It needs a warm, sunny spot and looks best against a soft background of foliage rather than a hard surface, which makes it a particularly useful plant to grow against a south-facing wall covered with spring- and early-summer-flowering climbers.

If you are looking for something exceptionally eye-catching for a conspicuous spot, you can't do much better than *Eremurus* (foxtail lily). This has very tall, 5–7 ft (1.5–2.1 m) pillars of flowers in bright yellow or orange, which look sensational firing up through the back of a traditional mixed border; even more so in a modern garden of interestingly shaped conifers and coloured-foliage shrubs. One particularly nice combination is the gold-filigreed *Chamaecyparis pisifera* 'Filifera Aurea', or burnished-orange *Thuja occidentalis* 'Rheingold', backed by deep-green foliage such as some of the ornamental pines with a group of foxtail lilies. They look well too with golden-leaved shrubs like the shaggy, cut-leaved elder, *Sambucus racemosus* 'Plumosa Aurea'. In a herbaceous border, try echoing their shape with red-hot pokers somewhere nearby. There is also a very soft-pink foxtail lily, *Eremurus robustus*, that associates wonderfully with tall blue or mauve delphiniums and old-fashioned roses. Eremurus lilies also go particularly well with conventional lilies in a border with lots of shrubby foliage. All eremurus can be a bit touchy to grow, and must have a very sunny, sheltered spot, with very well-drained soil containing plenty of organic matter. When you plant them, the peculiar roots, which look rather like a wagon wheel without the rim, should only be buried about 3 in (8 cm) deep, leaving the huge hen's-egg-sized growth bud in the centre protected by a thin covering of grit, coarse bark or similar material.

For an even more exotic look try *Tigridia pavonia*, another flower for a warm, sunny spot. But be warned – there is nothing remotely subtle about it. No one walking past tigridia can possibly overlook them; plant them where they can be seen from the road, and you'll have people knocking on your door asking what they are. Tigridias grow about 2 ft (60 cm) tall, with gladioli-like foliage, and flowers with three large triangular petals, often in iridescent blue or orange, with a central ring of a contrasting colour and usually heavily spotted. These are flowers to put in a place of honour, somewhere you will see them often. Use them to make a feature of a south-facing wall in front of a fan-trained fig tree, for a 'Continental holiday' look. Or add them to something with strong foliage shapes like fatsia, or coloured foliage combined with strong shapes like one of the purple or cream-and-pink-striped phormiums. Each startling tigridia flower lasts for only a day, but each stem produces a series of blooms over several consecutive days. Plant a good patch to make the most of them.

For sophistication, try another relatively unknown summer flower: galtonia (summer hyacinth). This is actually nothing like a normal hyacinth. The flowers are more like those of the hardy yucca, a tall spike of white dangling bell-shaped flowers, which can stand up to 3 ft (90 cm) high. The one most often seen in gardens is *Galtonia candicans*, which has white flowers. Flower arrangers, however, particularly appreciate the greeny flowers of *G. viridiflora*, and there is a more unusual species still, called *princeps*, which has flowers like bunches of green grapes. Galtonias are seen at their absolute best in a well-planned white border, where their striking shape contrasts well with fine-textured, silvery foliage such as that of artemesia. But they also make good additions to a normal mixed planting of herbaceous flowers and shrubs – anywhere a contrast in colour and shape is needed – so long as the situation is sunny and the soil is well drained. The same situation suits liatris, another flower with a very well-defined shape. Liatris has fluffy, 2–3-ft-(60–90-cm)-tall pokers of flower in pink, mauve or white, depending on the species, like giant pipe cleaners. It looks best with other striking plants that make the most of its extraordinary looks: *Salvia argentea* and *diascia*, or shrubs with reddish foliage, like *Berberis thunbergii* 'Rose Glow'.

CONTAINERS

Annuals may be the most popular container plants for patios, but a few judiciously placed summer-flowering bulbs amongst them do wonders for the display by making a contrast in shape and height. Tuberous begonias are the best-known summer bulb for containers; they flower continuously

Left: Crocosmia are traditional favourites for a herbaceous border though there is plenty of scope for experimenting with them in more adventurous plant associations too. Try them with conifers, bamboos and grasses for an interesting effect.

Below: Gladiolus can be grown in groups in a border, but if you want quantities for cutting, they are best planted in rows in the vegetable garden where you can cut them all without spoiling your display.

Eremurus, the foxtail lily, looks good in a large border where its rocket-like spikes can 'fire up' through shrubs or roses. *Eremurus elwessii* (here) has white flowers.

The loudest flowers In the garden – that's tigridia. In a warm, sunny, well-drained spot, they'll be the centre of attention.

throughout the summer, so they can be planted directly into tubs with annuals. You càn also get pendulous begonias, with clusters of smaller but otherwise similar flowers and a trailing habit, for hanging baskets. Both team up well with small-flowered annuals, and look all the better for a few foliage plants, such as helxine, or white flowers, such as *Lobelia* 'White Lady', to break up the mass of colour. You can use the same sort of scheme to create fashionable one-colour baskets, or matching baskets and tubs for a thoroughly coordinated-looking patio.

There are, however, many more unusual bulbs you could choose for containers, and different ways of using them. But, since few summer bulbs flower continuously all through the summer, it is a good idea to grow a succession of different kinds in separate containers, and treat them as temporary plants to add to your planting scheme when they look their best.

The larger bulbs often make good specimen plants; agapanthus looks well grown this way. It is a rather graceful plant with foliage similar to that of hippeastrum. Different cultivars are available, growing anything from 2–5 ft (60–150 cm) tall, topped by large heads of drooping tubular blue or white flowers in late summer. A large pot of tall agapanthus looks superb combined with a tub of fluffy blue ageratum, or a mixture of petunias containing a fair proportion of blue flowers. The agapanthus blooms dangle umbrella-like over the rest of the display, giving them a semi-tropical look.

Another interesting combination is to team large tubs of summer bulbs with pot-grown specimen shrubs. Lilies, such as the different forms of *L. tigrinum* (tiger lily), *pumilum*, a shorter species with vivid orange reflexed flowers, and the exotic-looking pink-and-white-spotted *speciosum* cultivars, all make good pot subjects. Team them with a large potted shrub like *Yucca filamentosa* or *Trachycarpus fortunei* (Chinese windmill palm) to create a nice Mediterranean feeling. Or, for a more tropical-looking planting, try canna. The plants are incredibly exotic-looking, with beautiful foliage, often reddish-purple or bronze, and huge yellow, orange, red or extravagantly spotted flowers, up to 5 in (13 cm) across. Plants grow 3–4 ft (90–120 cm) tall and associate well with other tropical-looking plants like castor oil plants, hardy yucca, potted lemon trees or hardy palms.

Another attractive idea is to add pot-grown bulbs to a permanent patio planting. Try planting a permanent group of dwarf conifers into the patio itself by removing a group of three paving slabs to make a small bed. Junipers withstand poor conditions quite well and are often grown this way. A good combination of conifers for this sort of arrangement would be: one low spreading juniper such as *Juniperus horizontalis* 'Turquoise Spreader', one with a bushy shape like *J. squamata* 'Chinese Silver', and one tall upright grower such as 'Skyrocket' – all in shades of blue. Or for a different colour scheme try a gold upright juniper such as *J. communis* 'Golden Showers' with the spreading *J.* × *media* 'Old Gold'. You can use the same basic conifer grouping throughout the year with a succession of different potted bulbs. In midsummer, you could have lilies as your seasonal highlights, with agapanthus in late summer. And, to fill the gap between the last of the lilies and the first of the agapanthus, how about eucomis (pineapple lily)? As the name suggests, the flower looks just like a greenish pineapple perched on a short spike above the foliage: very eye-catching.

ROCKERIES, RAISED BEDS AND SINK GARDENS

Summer is a good time for small bulbs that like sunny, well-drained conditions; several very unusual and interesting kinds are in flower then. As always with dwarf rockery plants, they look best planted in groups – individually they are too small to attract much attention. Many repay close inspection, so are best planted where they can be easily seen without your having to bend down too much, or step onto the rock garden to see them properly.

Some of the most fascinating in close-up are the dwarf alliums. *Allium cernuum* has foliage rather like clumps of chives with bright pink, nodding flowers grouped in clusters at the top of the stems, which may be 12–18 in (20–45 cm) tall. Another most attractive one is *A. pulchellum*. This has slightly curving stems topped by loose heads of lilac-pink flowers on long flower stalks, which give them a rather loose, shaggy appearance. Both species are inexpensive enough to plant them in quantity; they look superb associated with low, silvery plants like *Leucanthemum hosmariense*, or hovering above clumps of pinky flowers like *Geranium cinereum* 'Laurence Flatman' or 'Ballerina', amongst dwarf conifers. *Allium oreophilum*, another pink-flowered allium, at 6 in (15 cm) high, and even cheaper to buy, looks most striking planted as a June-flowering carpet between other plants. It is particularly effective with dwarf conifers, pieces of craggy rock and other miniature plants with interesting shapes.

Where you want a patch of brightly coloured flowers that continue for most of the summer, try rhodohypoxis. These tiny plants – only a few inches high – have foliage like short chunky grass, but you'd never notice as they are entirely smothered with inch-wide, starburst-shaped flowers. Many named varieties of *Rhodohypoxis baurii* are available, in brilliant red, pink or white. They are not hardy, so are best grown in pots and stood in a frost-free greenhouse in

winter, and sunk into place in the rockery when the foliage starts to appear in late spring. (You can of course keep them under glass for the summer if you prefer.) Team them with the small black-leaved *Ophiopogon planiscapus* 'Nigrescens', for an interesting contrast in shape and colour.

Sisyrinchiums are interesting plants, a bit like strange miniature irises, to which they are related. *Sisyrinchium striatum* looks very much at home in a rockery overlooking a pond, as the foliage is reminiscent of the water iris, although the flower is very different. It produces bolt-upright flower stems about 18 in (45 cm) high, studded at regular intervals with cream and yellow flowers – very striking. The smaller sisyrinchiums are mostly about 4 in (10 cm) tall, and look lovely when grown in large groups between other plants with contrasting foliage shapes or flower colours. *S. bellum* has bluish-green foliage and open-faced, pale purple flowers that look very much like violets from a distance. *S. brachypus* has yellow flowers and tends to seed itself about rather freely, but is nevertheless pretty. Both flower over the whole summer.

Another distinctly unusual flower is *Anomatheca cruenta* (syn. *Lapeirousia laxa*, *L. cruenta*) which should be much better known. The plant is like a small gladiolus, 6–8 in (15–20 cm) high, with loose sprays of incredibly pretty, salmon pink flowers ½ in (1 cm) across, each with a deeper salmon blotch in the centre. These plants look well

Tiger lilies make spectacular pot plants. Stand them on the patio or plunge them into the border wherever a splash of colour is needed.

Lilium speciosum cultivars flower in late summer – plant three bulbs in a 12–14 inch (30–35 cm) pot for a good display.

One of the more unusual summer-flowering bulbs is eucomis or pineapple flower. It certainly lives up to its name!

in a rockery, or in a sink garden, seen against a dark background. Try it with the very slow-growing dwarf conifer *Cryptomeria japonica* 'Vilmoriniana', which makes a compact knobbly shape and has slightly russet-tinged foliage, or delicate silvery foliage such as mounds of *Artemisia schmidtiana* 'Nana'. Although anomatheca is not the easiest bulb to acquire in the first place, once you have it, more plants are quickly raised from seed. If they are well cared for, seedlings can flower in their first year.

Finally, for a really spectacular rockery bulb, you cannot beat dierama. Its common name of angel's fishing rod really does it justice. The extraordinary flowers look just like a group of small purple anglers' floats

Above: Rhodohypoxis baurii hybrids are best grown in pots and plunged into the rockery for the summer as the bulbs are not hardy. Otherwise, leave them inside to decorate the greenhouse. They flower off and on for most of the summer.

Left: For the base of a rock garden, especially overlooking water, *Sisyrinchium striatum* is a good choice. Team it with lime green foliage such as the golden feverfew, as here, for an interesting combination.

suspended 3–4 ft (90–120 cm) up in mid-air by invisible threads. Dierama is grown at Wisley in a rock garden beside a small pond, where the flowers dangle down over the water accentuating its strange appearance. But it also makes a very spectacular centre-piece for a sunny, well-drained corner of the garden, dangling over low-growing plants or out over paving. The variety most commonly available is *Dierama pulcherrimum,* but there is little to choose between this and *D. pendulum,* or hybrids between the two; the general effect is the same, so get whichever you can.

WILD AND WOODLAND GARDENS

Although it is normally spring bulbs that come to mind for naturalising in wild and woodland gardens, some of the summer-flowering kinds can be used very success-fully to contribute to the unique atmosphere of this type of garden. The best-known of these are lilies. Most lilies will do well in a woodland clearing with their tops in sun and the base of the plant shaded by surrounding foliage, though some thrive in dappled shade under a light canopy of trees.

There is no reason why you shouldn't use hybrid lilies in this sort of situation, if you want to. (Choose those the catalogues describe as suitable for light shade.) Those with vivid orange flowers, which can be difficult to place in a more formal setting, look particularly good against a dark shady woodland background, to which they add an almost luminous presence. Or, in a small garden, try placing a group of bright orange lilies with a weeping birch and a small group of rhododendrons. *Lilium pardalinum* (panther lily), with bright orange, recurved flowers with black spots, and the large form of the tiger lily, *L. tigrinum* 'Splendens', which has large heads of orange flowers with black spots, both grow well in acid soil and partial shade. Or try planting a large drift of *L. martagon* in shades of pink, mauve and white. These look lovely naturalised in light shade under trees or amongst large shrubs, with their tall stems and recurved, lantern-like flowers.

For something really incredible, grow the giant Himalayan lily. This used to be known as *Lilium giganteum* but is now found under the name of *Cardiocrinum giganteum* in catalogues. A woodland garden, with acidic leaf-mould-rich soil and a sheltered situation, is about the only place to grow this successfully; and the only place it looks at home – the plant has stems 9–12 ft (2.7–3.6 m) tall, each bearing several large white flowers with red throats. Individual bulbs are expensive and short-lived but, once you have some, they propagate themselves from offsets and you can collect seed and produce more replacements.

For naturalising in damp grassland in sun or shade, try camassia. The best known is *Camassia esculenta*, which is commonly called quamash. The plant originates from North America, where the bulbs were eaten as a vegetable by Red Indians, and this was their name for it. Plants produce flower spikes about 1 ft (30 cm) high, each clad with deep blue, starry blooms in June. Plant quamash in clumps to accentuate a feature such as a seat, or use it more lavishly in drifts.

CUT FLOWERS

Of the summer bulbs, the only ones that you are likely to need in quantity for cutting are gladioli. For convenience, these are best grown in rows in the vegetable garden where the tall stems can be individually tied up to canes to keep them straight. By planting a short row of corms every two weeks from early March to late May, you will have gladioli to cut throughout the summer. For arranging, the smaller, more delicate butterfly gladioli are often preferred nowadays to the very heavy, formal-looking spikes of the large-flowered hybrids. A good range of colours are available including green. (Don't forget: gladioli corms need to be lifted and stored in a frost-free place for the winter.)

However, a lot of the most interesting

summer bulbs for cutting are the more unusual ones that you are more likely to want to grow in the border and pick a few at a time. The flowers most sought after for arranging are generally those with particularly striking shapes. For spherical shapes, the alliums are particular favourites, especially the ones with large flower heads like *A. giganteum* and *A. albopilosum*, and the rather more delicate *A. sphaerocephalum*. For spiky shapes, liatris is always in demand for cutting, with its fluffy, poker-like blooms in pink, mauve or white. For large trumpet shapes, many of the lilies are useful. If you want lilies for cutting, you might like to grow those found in florists, such as 'Stargazer' and 'Enchantment'. *L. longiflorum*, the one with huge ghostly white trumpets, can be grown but poses problems as it is not hardy; it is best grown in pots and stored in the greenhouse or conservatory for the winter.

There is no reason why you should not cut any lilies you have enough of to take without spoiling the look of the garden; tiger lilies look sensational in a vase. (Florists usually remove the stamens from lilies to prevent them shedding pollen onto furnishings, as it stains.) You can also take a few flowers from lesser-known summer bulbs that are good for cutting: galtonia, for instance, of which the green-flowered species are particularly sought after by arrangers, and acidanthera, which is nicely scented.

There is one flower that is very commonly seen in florists', and yet rarely grown in gardens: alstroemeria. This is so useful for cutting and is well worth the effort of finding plants and growing your own. *Alstroemeria* 'Ligtu Hybrids' and the species *pulchella* and *aurantiaca* are sometimes available. They should be treated as herbaceous plants and left undisturbed to form clumps, which will, in time, produce plenty of flowers for cutting. In winter, the plants are cut back and the roots covered with peat or bracken to give them some protection. (The sort you buy in the florist's are different varieties forced under glass to make them available all the year round; this isn't practical to do at home.)

HOUSE AND CONSERVATORY

Summer is probably the most exciting season of all for indoor bulbs. Of the more popular kinds, tuberous begonias and gloxinias are always good value as they flower continuously throughout the summer. Some of the lilies can also be grown in pots – *Lilium speciosum* cultivars with their huge pink- or red-spotted white flowers are commonly available just coming into flower from florists. The same lily bulbs can be pot-grown again in following years, or planted out in the garden after the flowers are over.

A woodland garden is the best place to grow the giant Himalayan lily, *Cardiocrinum giganteum*. It needs a cool, shady, sheltered spot with acidic soil, and associates well with hardy ferns, rhododendrons and banks of tall wildflowers, as well as more cultivated company.

Above: At Wisley, angel's fishing rod, or dierama, make a sensational addition to a small pond, grown so its flowers hang down over the water. *Below*: Exotic summer-flowering indoor bulbs, such as the climbing *Gloriosa rothschildiana* make interesting specimens for a conservatory.

Examples are gloriosa, eucharis and haemanthus, whose flamboyant blooms associate well with tropical foliage plants in large displays in a disused fireplace, on a low table or in parts of the conservatory where they are shaded from bright sunlight. The same plants also make good single specimens for growing in a place of honour, in a pretty pot cover. As they come from hot countries, these plants need to be treated with care. While they are in growth they must be kept in a warm room and not overwatered, as they tend to rot easily. Even when dormant it is essential the bulbs are stored somewhere warm (60°F/15°C minimum) and not put out in the greenhouse – even a frost-free one. You'll find all these bulbs offered in the spring catalogues of both large and small firms, and they are

SPECTACULAR EXOTICS

But besides these, there are several not-so-well-known summer-flowering bulbs, including some that are positively exotic which deserve to be much more available.

fascinating to experiment with. Each one has a distinct personality of its own.

Eucharis grandiflora, at first glance, look rather like narcissi; the flowers are about the same size, with a collar of white petals round a greenish-yellow cup. They are sweetly scented and appear at odd times during the summer. Each bulb can produce several flushes of flower, so don't think they are over after the first few – wait until autumn before reducing the watering.

Ismene is another exotic summer-flowering bulb; this is sometimes called Peruvian daffodil, and the flowers do bear some slight similarity to those of a trumpet daffodil. The trumpet is much wider open than a real daffodil's though, and the petals are very narrow – the whole character of the flower is much more exotic. Two kinds of ismene are readily available: *Ismene festivalis* which has white flowers, and a yellow cultivar called 'Sulphur Queen'. Both flower in early summer.

Haemanthus kalbreyeri has even more remarkable flowers. It is similar to a giant allium and has a large round head of red tubular flowers whose stamens grow outwards, giving a bristly effect like an overgrown shaving brush. The flowers are produced on top of a short stem protruding from amongst attractive foliage: a striking and unusual plant for a sunny window sill.

The climbing lily, *Gloriosa rothschildiana*, makes a sensational plant for a well-lit room or warm conservatory, given something to climb up. It can be allowed to ramble up trellis fixed to the wall of a conservatory, or up through a cane spiral of the sort used for many indoor plants. It does not need training or tying as it clings with its own tendrils which grow from the tips of the long, narrow, lily-like leaves. The large bright orange flowers are very much like martagon lilies to look at, with their reflexed petals and long elegant curving anthers. Gloriosa can be tricky to grow, but the secret is to plant the tubers in spring in a well-drained compost (John Innes with extra grit) and then keep them fairly warm and dry. That way, they'll come through with no problems. Water very sparingly until the plant is growing vigorously. And, from then on, to keep it growing steadily, feed gloriosa regularly and take care not to let the compost dry right out. If it suffers a check in growth at any time, it has a tendency to become dormant, and may do so before flowering. The only thing to do if its leaves start to yellow is gradually reduce the feeding and watering and let it go dormant just as you normally would in the autumn. Then keep the tubers completely dry until it is ready to resume growth the following year.

Another very 'different' flower is hedychium, the ginger lily. Several different species are occasionally available, but the most commonly found one is *Hedychium gardnerianum*. This grows about 4 ft (1.2 m) tall, with exotic foliage topped by a very elaborate, tropical-looking spike of yellow tubular flowers with long, red, protruding stamens, rather like a bottle-brush. The flowers appear in late summer, and very shortly after they are over the plant's stems start to snap away from the tuber without yellowing and drying out as most bulb foliage does. This can be a bit unnerving if you are not expecting it, but it is perfectly normal. When this happens, the tuber should be kept dry for the winter, and stored where the temperature remains above 45°F (7°C).

VICTORIAN FAVOURITES

Some unusual species of bulbs that look very exotic are not always so. These can put up with relatively low temperatures in winter and don't have to be kept in the house – they could be over-wintered in a frost-free greenhouse. Tuberoses were Victorian favourites; they produce spikes of highly scented, white flowers and used to be grown in special ornamental pots. Bulbs are occasionally available through catalogues: look for them under their Latin name, *Polianthes tuberosa*. The cultivar called 'The Pearl' is most often seen, and is nicest as it has double flowers. Unfortunately, tuberose bulbs are notorious for flowering so profusely they exhaust themselves, and won't then flower the following year. So, after the first flowering, grow them on in a frost-free greenhouse and build up the bulbs by regular feeding in the hope they will flower in alternate years. Otherwise, the best thing to do is to harden your heart and throw the old bulbs away after flowering, and buy new ones each year.

The arum lily is another exotic-looker that isn't so exotic to grow. The ordinary white arum lily, the sort that is sold as a cut flower at Easter, is *Zantedeschia aethiopica*, which is sometimes grown as a pot plant. This is virtually hardy, so presents no problem to grow in a cool conservatory. However, there are some other species with coloured flowers that are rather more exotic-looking. *Z. elliottiana*, for instance, has bright yellow flowers and dark green leaves which are usually heavily spotted with silver. *Z. rehmannii* has pink flowers and needs to be treated more carefully – it comes from Africa and must be kept warm at all times or the tuber will rot. Both are much smaller, weaker growers than *Z. aethiopica*, and therefore much more suitable as houseplants.

With such a wide variety of unusual and beautiful summer indoor bulbs available, why not give them a try, if you haven't already? You could soon find yourself a passionate collector.

4

GARDENING WITH BULBS:
AUTUMN AND WINTER

DESIGN GUIDELINES

As the season moves round to autumn, the summer flush of flowers draws to an end and the garden reverts to a landscape based on foliage. Given an Indian summer with warm, still weather, there may be a glorious show of autumn colour from trees such as acers and shrubs like fothergilla, which form the main attraction for a time. Eventually, though, deciduous trees and shrubs lose their leaves and herbaceous stems die back, leaving the bare bones of the winter landscape. Throughout this season flowers are in very short supply. So, to create a garden with all-year-round interest, it is vital to make the most of the limited flowering material that is available. The secret lies in grouping autumn and winter flowers effectively with architectural features and other plants that provide 'winter character' (evergreen foliage, coloured bark and so on) to create seasonal pockets of interest around the garden. This is where autumn-flowering bulbs prove invaluable; not just those that

start flowering late in the season such as autumn crocus and schizostylis, but those few later-summer-flowering kinds that continue into the autumn, like some cultivars of hemerocallis and agapanthus.

As the weather will still be quite warm at the end of the summer, you can design a series of autumn 'cameos', in much the same way as suggested for spring, with the aim of

Bulbs can still provide colour and variety as the season changes from summer to autumn.

leading you out into the garden. While the weather is still warm enough to spend time outside, plan your cameos to be walked around, and enjoy discovering different views when they are approached from different directions – there's no need to restrict yourself to a tight landscape round the house. But, as winter closes in, the main interest inevitably returns indoors, and all sorts of early spring flowers and other indoor bulbs can be used to bring the garden indoors. Use them with your existing foliage plants to create large displays; these can be re-designed as often as you want to create a fresh new look. Or, on a smaller scale, use impressive specimen plants or large bowls of bulbs as the centrepiece to a coffee table or window sill.

In spite of all their potential, the late-flowering bulbs are not very well known; surprising, when you think how important autumn and winter colour is in both house and garden. These bulbs play a vital part in forming the link between one season and the next, besides maintaining continuity of colour. So don't be put off by the unfamiliar names; look for them and grow them – you'll be amazed at the colour and character they add to what is all too often thought of as the 'dead end' of the gardening year.

BORDERS

Late summer and autumn are traditionally difficult times to maintain a colourful border. This is when you have to choose carefully, looking for flowers that span the awkward gap between seasons, as well as finding those that only begin their display late in the year, which help create a completely new character for the autumn garden.

TALL BULBS FOR GROWING IN GROUPS

Although lilies are mainly summer flowers, there are a few that flower in August and on into September. Of these, *Lilium speciosum* cultivars are specially eye-catching, with their big spotted flowers. *L.s.* 'Grand Commander' (deep pink flowers with red spots and white edges to the petals), 'Rubrum Magnificum' (white with a pink tinge and red spots) and 'Roseum' (pale pink with deeper pink spots) are all readily available. Plant them in small groups in a well-drained, sunny border, with tall, late herbaceous flowers such as *Macleaya cordata* (plume poppy), *Romneya coulteri* (tree poppy) which has large white poppy-like blooms, or pink or white Japanese anemones, for a really stunning display. Or grow the lilies in large pots and place them anywhere in a border that seems in need of a 'lift'. (Ensure the pots are stood amongst low-growing leaves or dwarf shrubs to keep the roots cool.)

Some of the most extraordinary-looking flowers for autumn interest are those of *Tricyrtis hirta* and *T. formosana stolonifera* (toad lilies). Though they are comparatively rarely grown, they deserve more popularity. Despite their off-putting common name, they have beautiful flowers that you need to look at in close-up really to appreciate the detail in each. The flowers, though individually small, grow in clusters at the top of 2 ft (60 cm) stems. Each bloom is halfway in appearance between a lily and an orchid and, depending on variety, they may be purplish, mauve or white and heavily spotted. They start appearing in August and September, and can continue into October. Even before they flower, toad lilies add interesting shapes and textures to the border – their flower stems have typical lily-like foliage which is often attractively mottled. Although related to lilies, tricyrtis do not grow from bulbs, but have thick tuberous roots. The plants grow best in much the same conditions as lilies – well-drained soil containing a lot of organic matter, and kept cool and shady round the roots. However, unlike most lilies, these plants prefer partial shade. Toad lilies look best grown in front of variegated foliage shrubs, or light, feathery flowers such as those of cimicifuga. *Cimicifuga ramosa* 'Atropurpurea', though an expensive plant to buy, has purplish foliage that complements toad lilies particularly well. Toad lilies also look good growing in groups with the purple bark of *Salix daphnoides*, or in shady pockets amongst evergreen hardy ferns. Try them with *Asplenium scolopendrium* (hart's tongue fern) or its strange crested form *A.s.* 'Crispum'.

Another all-too-rarely-seen autumn flower is schizostylis (Kaffir lily, but not to be confused with clivia, the indoor bulb that shares the same common name). Schizostylis' flowers look like miniature gladioli, but their 2 ft (60 cm) spikes of trumpet-shaped blooms are less formal and the flowers open out much wider. The most commonly seen is *S. coccinea* which has large bronzy-red flowers. Pink-flowered cultivars like the beautiful shell-pink 'Mrs Hegarty' can occasionally be found. Schizostylis are particularly valuable as they are one of the last autumn flowers in bloom, lasting from September well into November. They are easy to grow, liking any reasonably well-sheltered, sunny situation with moist soil. But, being so striking, they are not easy flowers to place. They are seen to best advantage against a plain background of evergreen foliage; grow a good-sized clump amongst evergreens with neat domed shapes such as *Choisya ternata*, or the rough-textured foliage of *Viburnum rhytidophyllum*. You could also try grouping a patch of *S. coccinea* with a pyracantha or cotoneaster with berries of the same colour. Or, more spectacular still, try either the red of pink cultivars with a shrub grown for its late autumn tints like *Nyssa sylvatica*, which combines red, orange and yellow.

CARPETING BULBS

Autumn-flowering crocuses and colchicums are roughly the same shape and size

Agapanthus joins other late-summer and early-autumn-flowering plants, such as *Sedum spectabile* and silver-foliaged artemesia, to give good late display.

Lilium speciosum rubrum has beautiful pink spotted flowers in August and September. It can be grown in the garden, in pots on the patio, in a conservatory or indoors.

as spring crocuses. Different varieties of colchicum are available in shades of pink, mauve or cream, often with heavily chequered patterns; crocuses have the same colour range with the addition of blue. Both are available cheaply in mixtures, specially for naturalising, or separately as named varieties. Sternbergia is another crocus-like flower. Only one variety, *Sternbergia lutea*, which has yellow flowers, is commonly available.

To make the most of such small flowers in the garden, it is a good idea to group them in

Schizostylis are valuable for providing an autumn display. 'Mrs Hegarty' (here) flowers right through to November in a good year.

associate particularly well with yellow-berried shrubs such as *Pyracantha rogersiana* 'Flava'. Try clumps of any yellow-, cream-, pink- or mauve-flowered bulbs, or a mixture of colours, grown with *Callicarpa bodinieri giraldii* – this is an unusual shrub with purple berries that remain on the bare branches for a time after the leaves have fallen. The same colours also go well with symphoricarpos (snowberry), which has either pink or white berries depending on the variety. 'Mother of Pearl' is one of the best cultivars, and has slightly pink-flushed, white berries – these look

A lot of small autumn-flowering bulbs look very similar to crocus, but with the flowers appearing before the foliage. These are *Colchicum autumnale*, which look good naturalised amongst conifers in a well-drained spot.

small carpets with evergreens and conifers, shrubs grown for winter bark colours like salix and dogwoods, or colourful autumn foliage or berries. They could also be planted in grass under specimen trees and shrubs. You can plan autumn cameos round a particular colour scheme, such as blue and lilac or pink and mauve, or go for an altogether more colourful effect by teaming a multicoloured carpet of bulbs with a nice specimen tree or shrub.

CARPETING BULBS WITH BERRYING SHRUBS

Autumn berries always look good grown with autumn bulbs. Purple or blue crocuses particularly impressive seen against a carpet of pink, purple and cream.

CARPETING BULBS WITH EVERGREEN FOLIAGE

With conifers or evergreens, use different-coloured groups of dwarf bulbs to light up odd corners between plants, interspersed with occasional larger carpets to vary the pattern of the planting scheme. The small flowers contrast beautifully with the texture of the foliage, and the brilliant colours really stand out against the dark background. Blue and gold foliage benefit most from the bright colours; try a group of brilliant yellow *Sternbergia lutea* at the foot of a gold or variegated conifer, or the pale pink of *Crocus speciosus* planted with pale blue conifers like *Chamaecyparis pisifera* 'Boulevard'. If you like more spectacular flowers, choose the luminous rosy-carmine of *Colchicum speciosum* 'Lilac Wonder', or the softer pink double-flowered *C.s.* 'Waterlily', to go with grey or blue conifers. Both also look good grown at the foot of a specimen tree planted amongst evergreens, such as birch or *Acer griseum*, where autumn interest is provided by the bark.

CARPETING BULBS WITH AUTUMN LEAVES

Autumn foliage tints associate surprisingly well with dwarf bulbs of any colour. Plant a few groups of crocuses, colchicums or sternbergia under *Rhus cotinus*, fothergilla or enkianthus, or under small trees, like *Nyssa sylvatica*, amelanchier, liquidambar and acers, that produce good autumn colours. The red and gold foliage makes an even prettier picture after it has fallen, with the flowers nosing up through the carpet of multicoloured leaves.

The autumn-flowering hardy cyclamen species, *Cyclamen neapolitanum* and *C. purpurascens*, look good grown in carpets under shrubs or trees too, but the pink flowers are so small that they are easily buried by falling leaves. They look best grown under trees like birches that have only a light canopy of small leaves to shed.

WELL-DRAINED BORDERS IN FRONT OF SOUTH-FACING WALLS

A lot of gardens have a small border of this sort, often under the windows at the front of the house. Frequently, the bed is narrow, bordering a wall on one side and a path on the other, so it is very dry, as well as hot and sunny, in summer – conditions that can be very difficult to find suitable plants for. However, it is tailor-made for two particularly exotic autumn-flowering bulbs: *Nerine bowdenii* and *Amaryllis belladonna*.

Nerine bowdenii is rather an odd plant in that it produces leaves in spring which die down towards the end of summer, leaving the flowers to appear from bare soil in the autumn (accounting for their common name of naked ladies). The flowers are large and spectacular, bright pink with long narrow petals that curl back at the tips. The amaryllis is not the one we grow as a pot plant, which should, correctly speaking, be called hippeastrum, though the flowers are not dissimilar. *Amaryllis belladonna* has large clusters of big lily-like flowers in mauvish-pink with white throats, which come out any time in September and October. The bulbs should be left undisturbed to form clumps. Both plants grow better on their own, without anything else competing with them. Their large, colourful flowers and strong shapes look most dramatic seen alone against a background of soil, with a plain brick or colour-washed wall behind.

CONTAINERS

In autumn, your patio tubs and planters will probably not be available to use as they'll be planted with spring-flowering bulbs. But you can grow some autumn-flowering bulbs in ordinary pots. These will look good grouped with a few potted conifers or evergreens. Or, if you have the same plants set into a bed within the patio, you could simply stand a few pots with them for a temporary splash of colour.

Schizostylis grow well in pots, and are tall enough to make a good display. You may also have a few of the later-flowering agapanthus to use; most flower in August, but some cultivars, such as 'Bressingham Blue' and 'Blue Giant', keep flowering well into September. Most of your colour, however, will come from much smaller bulbs, like autumn crocuses, colchicums and sternbergia. Here, it may be worth reserving one or two of your large patio planters specially for them. Simply leave the old compost in the container or fill it with peat, and plunge several pots of autumn-flowering bulbs temporarily into them. (The same containers can then be used later for plunging pot-grown polyanthus.)

Alternatively, grow small bulbs in shallow alpine pans or ornamental terracotta pots and stand them in informal groups on the sides of brick or stone steps, or on top of a low wall where they'll make a good display. You could use any of the species recommended for naturalising in borders in this way. But to that list you could also add a rather unusual bulb called zephyranthes. Its common names, flower of the west wind and zephyr lily, suggest eastern promise, though the flowers are, like those of many autumn bulbs, rather similar to those of the crocus. Two kinds of zephyr lily appear in the catalogues: *Zephyranthes candida*, which has white flowers; and *Z. robusta*, by far the prettier, which is a lovely clear pink but unfortunately not hardy so bulbs must be taken under cover for winter. Both species must have very good drainage, so give them a compost of John Innes potting with extra grit added.

Autumn-flowering bulbs and fallen leaves make an attractive combination. Here, *Crocus speciosus* is naturalised at the edge of a lawn.

Nerine bowdenii is hardy outdoors in a sheltered spot, but needs the protection of a south-facing wall. It flowers in the autumn, after the foliage has died down.

Amaryllis belladonna is another exotic looking flower for a south-facing border at the foot of a wall. Like nerine, it grows best without other plants that might smother its leaves.

Left: 'Waterlily' is one of the most popular colchicums. It makes an eyecatching plant for indoors – in a pot or simply standing in a saucer – and it can also be naturalised out in the garden, given a sunny, well-drained spot. Try it in a rock garden or with shrubs like *Symphoricarpos* 'Mother of Pearl' for an interesting combination.

Bottom left: *Tricyrtis stolonifera*, the toad lily, is a little-known late summer/autumn flower that deserves to be much more widely grown.

Above: Zephyranthes (flower of the west wind) are lovely autumn-flowering bulbs for containers or a rock garden. The white-flowered *candida* is hardy, but the choicer *robusta* shown here needs keeping in a frost-free greenhouse for the winter.

ROCKERIES, RAISED BEDS AND SINK GARDENS

Any of the autumn crocuses, colchicums, sternbergia and zephyranthes already mentioned can be grown in this sort of situation. But, unlike in the open garden where you need a carpet of dwarf bulbs to make a good show, in the confines of a rockery, raised bed or sink, a few dozen are enough to create a worthwhile display as the flowers are raised up and therefore easier to see. They'll automatically have a good background, in the shape of stone chippings or rocks, and possibly dwarf conifers or other evergreen rock plants. The flowers will also last better, given the sheltered situation normally chosen for this type of garden feature. And, particularly if the soil in the main garden is heavy, you'll stand a much better chance of growing autumn-flowering bulbs successfully here, since the free drainage provides much better conditions.

Most small bulbs can be planted in groups amongst dwarf conifers and other evergreens that provide a good background, and left permanently in place. The non-hardy *Zephyranthes robusta*, however, is best grown in small groups in a pot, and just plunged in position in summer. After flowering, it should be removed to the protection of a greenhouse. The autumn-flowering *Cyclamen purpurascens* and *C. hederifolium* can also be planted on the rockery; although they like leaf-mould-rich soil, they also need a site that does not become waterlogged in winter, so a leafy pocket of soil in a cool spot in partial shade suits them well. Grow them with miniature evergreen ferns, which like the same conditions.

However, if you already have a lot of naturalised autumn-flowering bulbs growing elsewhere in the garden, you would probably prefer to reserve these choicer planting sites for something a bit more special. Generally these will be the more expensive bulbs, and those which repay particular attention, or insist on specially good drainage. Into this category come *Colchicum speciosum* 'Waterlily', which has huge lilac-pink double flowers, and *C. aggripinum*, which is scarce but worth looking out for on account of its unusual flowers which are very heavily chequered in three colours – pink, purple and white. (This incidentally associates particular well with the colours of autumn leaves.) Of the crocuses, *Crocus sativus* (saffron crocus) is an interesting curiosity. It has large lilac- and violet-marked flowers, from which the anthers were once harvested and dried to produce culinary saffron. You'd need to plant a lot to collect a worthwhile quantity of saffron, but it's fun to know that you could. You might also try the scarce *Sternbergia clusiana*, which has large and brighter yellow flowers than *S. lutea*, and they open into a perfect globular shape.

CUT FLOWERS

The very end of summer and early autumn are notoriously poor times for flower arrangers who rely on material to cut from the garden. The summer flowers are either over or not in sufficiently perfect condition for cutting, yet it is too early for the autumn colours, bare branches and late winter/early spring flowers. There are, however, a few bulbs that fill the gap nicely. Late-flowering agapanthus, such as 'Bressingham Blue' and 'Blue Giant', will still be available into September, and all produce good seed-heads for cutting in any case. Schizostylis make good cut flowers, and you can also cut any lilies and nerines. But, with all of these, you need to grow plenty to be sure of having enough to cut without decimating the garden display. Another good candidate for cutting is the late-flowering *Hemerocallis* 'Stella d'Oro', which, though only 2 ft (60 cm) tall, does continue producing its yellow flowers right through to the first frost. Other good hemerocallis cultivars that flower into September, and have the unusual colours loved by arrangers, include 'Chartreuse Magic' (yellow and green flowers), 'Bonanza' (orange and brown flowers), 'Giant Moon' (yellow with white stripes) and 'Nob Hill' (pink, yellow and cream). *Liatris callilepis*, which has lilac-purple, poker-like flowers, is another bulb that goes on into September and has a lot of uses for arrangers.

One of the most fascinating sorts of material for flower arrangers is seed-heads, and in autumn *Iris foetidissima* (gladwyn) produces its large pods which split open to reveal rows of orange, pea-like berries. Although not technically a bulb, this is a species of iris with thick tuberous roots that is usually sold as a growing plant rather than a dormant root. It is particularly useful in the garden as it grows in any poor, shady spot, the leaves forming attractive evergreen fans, although the pale blue flowers in spring are insignificant. Try gladwyn seed-heads in a vase with late-flowering kniphofia (red-hot poker). Cultivars, such as 'Little Maid' (2 ft/60 cm tall, yellow and cream poker-like flowers) and 'Bressingham Comet' (2 ft/60 cm tall, red and yellow pokers), can all flower into October given a good autumn. 'Percy's Pride' (2 ft/60 cm tall, yellow and green pokers) will often continue into December if the weather stays mild. Similarly, in a mild winter, you may find the winter-flowering *Iris unguicularis* starting to bloom from as early as late November. If this happens, it is frankly best to pick the flowers just as the buds show their true colour, for any sudden change in the weather will spoil them if they are left in the garden, and you'll do much better to have them safely indoors.

HOUSE AND CONSERVATORY

Meanwhile, indoors, another completely different set of bulbs are well on the way to creating a new season's display. And when

Sternbergia lutea makes a nice touch of gold that goes well with variegated foliage.

Hardy cyclamen like autumn-flowering *Cyclamen hederifolium* make a good carpet in light shade under trees, but make sure they aren't buried by fallen leaves. Try them in shady, leafmould-rich pockets in a rock garden too.

Left: The winter flowering *Iris unguicularis* needs a south-facing wall to grow well. Given mild weather it may start to bloom at the end of November. Since the flowers are quite fragile, they are safer picked and put in a vase than left out in the garden. This is the cultivar 'Mary Barnard' which has rather larger flowers than the species.

Agapanthus are bulbs no keen gardener should be without. They are useful as late summer flowers in pots on the patio, in borders and for cutting. Choose cultivars such as 'Bressingham Blue' and 'Blue Giant' which continue flowering into September.

Another useful late summer flower is liatris. Again it is as useful for cutting as it is in the garden, so grow plenty!

there is so little going on in the garden outdoors, it is worth making a special effort to create an interesting and varied landscape indoors.

PERMANENT INDOOR BULBS

Vallota (Scarborough lily) flowers in late summer and early autumn. It has large, striking, red, lily-like blooms at the top of thick, fleshy stems about 1 ft (30 cm) high. The foliage is similar to that of hippeastrum, and grows about the same size, so this is a plant for a large pot. Not so well known, but much more extraordinary-looking, is velthemia, a South African bulb with attractive, wavy-

edged leaves and flowers rather like a red-hot poker, but pink tinged with green. They appear during the winter just before or after Christmas. Coming from a dry climate, this plant needs watering rather sparingly during its growing season (winter) when it also needs to be kept fairly warm. In summer, it should be kept completely dry after the foliage has died back, until it starts growing again in early autumn. Both this and vallota are plants for a sunny window sill and, since they are both so imposing, they look best stood in a nice pot cover and used as specimen plants. However, you could add them to a group of the more robust-looking foliage pot plants, such as fatsia, fatshedera or asparagus fern, or to a collection of tropical ones with colourful leaves like maranta, to introduce seasonal flowers to the display.

OUTDOOR BULBS INDOORS

Besides the bulbs that are grown permanently indoors, the autumn and winter are a great time for outdoor bulbs grown indoors.

Pots of schizostylis can be brought into the conservatory to make a display. Particularly if the weather is inhospitable outside, then bringing them under cover will ensure the flowers keep in good condition for longer – outdoors the large petals tend to get quickly battered by the wind. Colchicums, too, can be brought indoors, but here you don't even need to grow them in pots. The bulbs can simply be sat in a saucer, where they will flower without any soil or water. The more spectacular varieties like the huge, double, lilac-pink-flowered 'Waterlily', or the luminous, rosy-magenta 'Lilac Wonder', are specially striking, though you can do the same with any colchicums. This is a fascinating way to introduce children to growing their own plants, as everything happens quite quickly and they can see exactly what is going on. Colchicums are not just fun to grow; you can also use the bulbs as the basis for quite a sophisticated display. You could fill a pretty glass dish, an old-fashioned cake stand perhaps, with bulbs, or use them as a sort of 'pot et fleur' arrangement with tropical foliage plants. Since they grow without

soil, you can also use them to try out some more unconventional ideas too. Try using them instead of airplants standing in small ornaments, or wired up into the branches of large specimen foliage plants like weeping fig. However, if you want the bulbs to grow again after flowering them dry, they should be planted out in the garden as soon as the flowers are over.

Following on a little later than colchicums come the very first of the early spring bulbs. Hyacinths, daffodils and sometimes even tulips are available that have been specially treated to persuade them to flower early; some can even be in flower before Christmas. You can buy bowls of bulbs just coming into bloom at garden centres, but it isn't difficult to grow your own. Make sure you buy bulbs described as specially prepared, as the normal ones won't flower nearly so early. Look out for them in garden centres and catalogues from the middle of August onwards. They'll probably be a little more expensive than normal, untreated bulbs.

If you want your plants to flower for Christmas, treated bulbs must be planted no later than the middle of September. Plant them individually in pots, or group several bulbs of the same kind together in bowls. The method of planting is exactly the same as for normal spring bulbs. Plants grown individually in pots can be stood inside an ornamental pot cover when you bring them indoors, or plunged into a large container to make a display either entirely of bulbs, or mixed with other indoor plants. Hyacinths can be grown in the special hyacinth glasses which are sometimes available. After they have finished flowering, treated bulbs can be gradually hardened off and planted out in the garden like normal bulbs, though they may take a year to recover before starting to flower again. They should not be forced again.

One group of bulbs deserves special mention. They are the Tazetta group of narcissi, which includes the well-known varieties 'Soleil d'Or' and 'Paper White'. These are amongst the first daffodils to bloom, and the sort commonly sold as early cut flowers. None of them is hardy enough to grow outside in the garden, but they do make very good flowering plants for indoors, and they are very much quicker and simpler to grow than normal spring bulbs. With Tazetta narcissi, there is no need to keep them outside until they are in bud, as you would with other spring bulbs. They flower within about eight weeks of planting, and you can either grow them the usual way – in compost or bulb fibre – or plant them in a bowl of pebbles, which makes quite a novelty. Choose plenty of smooth, pretty pebbles – they can be any size from gravel right up to bantam-egg size – and almost fill a clear bowl with them. Some people like to add a few pieces of horticultural charcoal (the sort sold for bottle gardens) to keep the pebbles sweet, but this is not essential. Don't bury the bulbs; just press them into position so they stand up on their own. Then water, filling the bowl so the water level comes to ½ inch (1 cm) below the base of the bulbs.

Keep the bowl somewhere cool, below 50°F (10°C) – it won't matter whether they are in the light or kept dark – until the flowers start to open, then move them wherever you like to enjoy the blooms. The cooler you keep them, however, the longer they'll last: 50–55°F (10–13°C) is ideal. After flowering, add a little liquid feed to the water while the foliage completes its growth cycle and dies away, then remove the bulbs and dry them to replant the next year. If you want flowers for Christmas, plant Tazetta narcissi in October. But, since bulbs are normally available from August or September onwards, why not plant some every two or three weeks for a continuous display leading up to Christmas too?

GREENHOUSE AND COLD FRAME

Under glass you can grow any of the bulbs already suggested for growing indoors or in containers outdoors. Both kinds last longer in a cool greenhouse; the outdoor sorts because they are protected from the weather, and the indoor ones because they are not too hot, as they often are in the house. In an unheated greenhouse, you could grow pots of schizostylis, autumn-flowering crocus and colchicums, and specially prepared spring bulbs like hyacinths,

The earlier 'spring' daffodils are those of Tazetta narcissi like the popular 'Soleil d'Or' shown here. Cut flowers are available in florists from November, but you can grow your own plants indoors on a window sill in a bowl of pebbles.

Above: The fragile *Narcissus bulbocodium romieuxii* is not often seen but easy to grow once you have bought the bulb.

Hyacinths which have been specially treated to make them flower early, can be in flower for Christmas provided they are planted in time. Try growing them in tanks of pebbles as an alternative to old-fashioned hyacinth glasses.

Opposite: The species *Cyclamen persicum* is much more delicate than the better known florists cyclamen, of which it is a parent. It is best grown in a frost-free greenhouse though it can be kept on a cool windowsill indoors.

tulips and daffodils. The shorter-growing crocus and colchicums could be grown in a cold frame if you prefer. To that list you could add an even more unusual bulb, the autumn-flowering snowdrop, *Galanthus reginae-olgae*. This flowers in October and, although the bulbs are scarce and expensive, it makes a fascinating curio. The flowers appear on their own, with the foliage following later. A pot of three or five bulbs is a fascinating sight at such an apparently unseasonal time but, at the price, even a single bulb in a pot is well worth growing. The autumn snowdrop is something of a collectors' bulb and normally only available from small specialist bulb firms.

Another enthusiasts' plant is the tiny autumn-flowering daffodil, *Narcissus bulbocodium romieuxii*. This grows about 4 in (10 cm) tall, with flowers like the more familiar spring-flowering *bulbocodium*, but in very pale yellow. The foliage is like slender grass, and the whole effect is very frail and delicate. Again, it is not often seen, but easily grown once you are able to buy the bulbs.

In a heated greenhouse (kept at a minimum temperature of 40°F/5°C) you could grow any of the *Narcissus tazetta* as well as the vallota and velthemia mentioned earlier for growing indoors. Since bulbs do not make very inspiring pot plants when they aren't in flower, a lot of people keep them in a heated greenhouse most of the time, and just take them indoors when they are in bloom.

The really sensational autumn-flowering bulbs for a frost-free greenhouse are nerines. Apart from the better-known *Nerine bowdenii*, which can be grown outside in a warm south-facing border, there are quite a few less common and very spectacular tender nerines, which can only be grown satisfactorily in a greenhouse. They include *N. sarniensis* (Guernsey lily) which has orange-red flowers, *N. crispa* which has pale pink flowers with curly tips to the petals, and named varieties of *N. bowdenii*, as well as a limited selection of hybrids in various shades of red, pink or white. These kinds of nerines are best grown in pots, and stood outside on the patio in summer. Since they only need to be kept just frost-free in winter, a minimum temperature of 32°F (0°C) is perfectly adequate. Plants could be moved temporarily indoors or into a conservatory while looking their best, but should be kept as cool as possible.

Species cyclamen are a very collectable group of plants. Some are certainly hardy, but they are better grown under glass where the corms are protected from winter wet, and their flowers from damaging cold wind. Some of the choicer species are not reliably hardy, and must have frost-free conditions. There is quite a large choice of species, with white, pink, or pink and mauve flowers. Many have beautifully patterned leaves.

One of the first to flower is *Cyclamen graecum*, which performs in September and October shortly after the new leaves have appeared. The flowers are pink, and the leaves are often attractively marbled with silver or a mixture of light and dark green. *C. cyprium* flowers in October, with highly scented white flowers. This is sometimes recommended for growing out of doors, but unless you provide a very well-drained, sheltered site, it is much safer grown under cold or frost-free glass. And, in an enclosed space out of the wind, you'll notice the perfume of the flowers much more. *C. africanum* flowers a little later, with flowers scented of violets. By growing one each of the autumn-flowering kinds, and following on with early spring species such as *C. persicum*, *C. libanoticum*, and the pewter-leaved selections of *C. coum*, you can have a most interesting collection which has something in flower for up to six months.

INFORMATIVE INDEX OF BULBS

KEY

Height – average height.

Situation – unless otherwise stated, bulbs need sun for at least half the day. Exceptions are marked: LS light shade; S–LS sun or light shade; SFW south-facing wall; SD very sunny and well drained.

Soil – unless otherwise stated, bulbs need well drained but moisture-retentive soil. Exceptions are marked: M moist; A acid; LT lime-tolerant; LH lime-hating (i.e. needs acid soil).

Plant – month when to plant.

Depth – depth of soil over top of bulb. 2X = twice depth of bulb; C just cover with soil/compost; S leave tip of bulb showing above surface; ½ = half bulb above compost.

Grow – brief growing instructions. FF frost-free; HH half-hardy, lift for winter; H house followed by minimum winter temperature where necessary; GH greenhouse or frame; L leave undisturbed to form clumps (i.e. naturalise); B treat as bedding; W protect with layer of peat or litter in winter; HB treat as herbaceous perennial; E evergreen or sometimes so (does not/may not become dormant).

Flowering – months when flowering (may vary slightly due to seasonal variation in weather). SC scented; X specially recommended for cutting.

NAME and COMMON NAME	HEIGHT	SITUATION	SOIL	PLANT	DEPTH	GROW	FLOWERING
Acidanthera murielae	3 ft (90 cm)	SFW		Apr–May	4 in (10 cm)	HH	Aug–Sept SC X
Agapanthus (African lily)							
patens 'Headbourne Hybrids'	2½ ft (75 cm)			Apr–May	2 in (5 cm)	HH	Jul–Aug X
africanus 'Bressingham Blue'	2½ ft (75 cm)			Apr–May	2 in (5 cm)	HH	Jul–Sept X
africanus 'Blue Giant'	3½ ft (100 cm)			Apr–May	2 in (5 cm)	HH	Jul–Sept X
Allium (ornamental onion)							
albopilosum	2 ft (60 cm)			Sept–Oct	3–4X	L	June X
bulgaricum							
(see *Nectaroscordum siculum bulgaricum*)							
cernuum	1 ft (30 cm)			Sept–Oct	3–4X	L	June–Jul
giganteum	4 ft (120 cm)			Sept–Oct	3–4X	L	June X
karataviense	1 ft (30 cm)			Sept–Oct	3–4X	L	June X
oreophilum	6 in (15 cm)			Sept–Oct	3–4X	L	June
pulchellum	1½ ft (45 cm)			Sept–Oct	3–4X	L	June–Aug
sphaerocephalum	1½ ft (45 cm)			Sept–Oct	3–4X	L	Jul–Aug X
Alstroemeria (Peruvian lily)							
'Ligtu Hybrids'	2½ ft (75 cm)			Mar–Apr	4–6 in (10–15 cm)	HW	June–Jul X
aurantiaca	3 ft (90 cm)			Mar–Apr	4–6 in (10–15 cm)	HW	Jul–Sept X
pulchella	3 ft (90 cm)			Mar–Apr	4–6 in (10–15 cm)	HW	Jul–Sept X
Amaryllis belladonna	2 ft (30 cm)	SFW		June–Jul	6 in (15 cm)	L	Sept–Oct X

Name	Height	Position		Planting time	Depth	Hardiness	Flowering
Anemone							
blanda	3 in (7.5 cm)	S–LS		Sept–Oct	2 in (5 cm)	L	Feb–Apr
coronaria 'De Caen'	8 in (20 cm)			Sept–May	2 in (5 cm)	L	Mar–Jul X
coronaria 'St Brigid'	8 in (20 cm)			Sept–May	2 in (5 cm)	L	Mar–Jul X
nemorosa (wood anemone)	6 in (15 cm)	LS		Sept–Oct	2 in (5 cm)	L	Mar–Apr
Anomatheca cruenta	8 in (20 cm)	SD		Apr–May	1 in (2.5 cm)	HH	Jul–Aug
Arum italicum 'Pictum'	6 in (15 cm)	S–LS		Aug–Sept	1 in (2.5 cm)	L	Winter foliage
Begonia: tuberous	1 ft (30 cm)			Mar–May	S	HH	Jul–Sept
Begonia: pendulous	1 ft (30 cm)			Mar–May	S	HH	Jul–Sept
Camassia esculenta (quamash)	1 ft (30 cm)	S–LS	M	Sept–Oct	4 in (10 cm)	L	June
Canna (Indian shot plant)	3–4 ft (90–120 cm)			May–Jun	C	HH	Jul–Sept
Cardiocrinum giganteum (giant Himalayan lily)	9–12 ft (270–360 cm)	S–LS	A	Oct	C	L	Jul–Aug
Clivia (Kaffir lily)	1 ft (30 cm)			Apr–May	½	HE	Apr
Colchicum							
aggripinum	4–6 in (10–15 cm)			Aug–Sept	3 in (7.5 cm)	L	Sept–Nov
speciosum 'Lilac Wonder'	4–6 in (10–15 cm)			Aug–Sept	3 in (7.5 cm)	L	Sept–Nov
speciosum 'Waterlily'	4–6 in (10–15 cm)			Aug–Sept	3 in (7.5 cm)	L	Sept–Nov
Convallaria majalis (lily of the valley)	4 in (10 cm)	LS		Sept–Oct	C	L	Apr–May SC X
Crocosmia (montbretia)	1½ ft (45 cm)			Apr	3 in (7.5 cm)	L W	June–Jul
Crocus (spring-flowering)	4 in (10 cm)			Sept–Oct	3 in (7.5 cm)	L	Mar
Crocus (autumn-flowering)							
sativus (Saffron crocus)	4 in (10 cm)			Aug–Sept	3 in (7.5 cm)	L	Oct
speciosus	4 in (10 cm)			Aug–Sept	3 in (7.5 cm)	L	Oct
Cyclamen – buy in pots while in growth, not as dry corms, leafy soil where planted in garden							
africanum	4–6 in (10–15 cm)	LS			½ – C	GH	Oct SC
coum	4–6 in (10–15 cm)	LS			½ – C	GH	Jan–Mar
coum 'Pewter' (silver-leaved form)	4–6 in (10–15 cm)	LS			½ – C	GH	Jan–Mar
cyprium	4–6 in (10–15 cm)	LS			½ – C	GH	Oct SC
graecum	4–6 in (10–15 cm)	LS			½ – C	FF GH	Sept–Oct
libanoticum	4–6 in (10–15 cm)	LS			½ – C	GH	Feb–Mar
neapolitanum	4–6 in (10–15 cm)	LS			½ – C	GH	Aug–Nov
persicum	4–6 in (10–15 cm)	LS			½	FF GH	Mar–Apr
purpurascens	4–6 in (10–15 cm)	LS			½		Aug–Sept SC
trochopteranthum	4–6 in (10–15 cm)	LS			½ – C	GH	Jan–Mar SC
Dierama (angel's fishing rod)							
pulcherrimum	3 ft (90 cm)			Sept or Apr	6 in (15 cm)	L W or B	Aug–Sept
pendulum	2 ft (30 cm)			Sept or Apr	6 in (15 cm)	L W or B	June–Jul
Endymion nonscriptus (bluebell)	8 in (20 cm)	S–LS		Sept–Oct	2 in (5 cm)	L	Apr–May
Eranthis hyemalis (winter aconite)	4 in (10 cm)	S–LS		Sept–Oct	1 in (2.5 cm)	L	Feb–Mar

NAME and COMMON NAME	HEIGHT	SITUATION	SOIL	PLANT	DEPTH	GROW	FLOWERING
Eremurus (foxtail lily)							
'Shelford Hybrids'	5-7 ft (150-210 cm)	SD		Sept-Oct	3 in (7.5 cm)	W	June-Jul X
robustus	8-10 ft (240-300 cm)	SD		Sept-Oct	3 in (7.5 cm)	W	June X
Erythronium							
dens-canis (dog's tooth violet)	4 in (10 cm)	LS	M	Sept-Oct	3 in (7.5 cm)	L	Apr
tuolumnense	10 in (25 cm)	LS	M	Sept-Oct	3 in (7.5 cm)	L	Apr
Eucharis grandiflora	1½ ft (45 cm)			Apr-May	S	H 60°F (15°C)	June-Aug SC
Eucomis bicolor (pineapple flower)	1 ft (30 cm)			Mar-Apr	C	HH	Jul-Aug
Freesia	1½ ft (45 cm)			Nov	S	FF GH	Mar-Apr X
Fritillaria							
acmopetala	15 in (38 cm)	SD		Sept-Oct	4 in (10 cm)	L	Apr
imperialis (crown imperial)	2 ft (60 cm)	S-LS		Sept-Oct	6 in (15 cm)	L	Apr-May
meleagris (snake's head fritillary)	1 ft (30 cm)	S-LS	M	Sept-Oct	4 in (10 cm)	L	Apr
meleagris 'Aphrodite'	1 ft (30 cm)	S-LS	M	Sept-Oct	4 in (10 cm)	L	Apr
michailovskii	6 in (15 cm)	SD		Sept-Oct	4 in (10 cm)	L	Mar-Apr
persica 'Adiyaman'	2 ft (60 cm)			Sept-Oct	4 in (10 cm)	L	May
Galanthus (snowdrop) – plant in the green after flowering if possible							
nivalis	6 in (15 cm)	LS		Sept-Oct	4 in (10 cm)	L	Jan-Mar
G.n. reginae-olgae	6 in (15 cm)			Mar-Apr	C	GH	10
Galtonia (summer hyacinth)							
candicans	3 ft (90 cm)	SD		Mar-Apr	6 in (15 cm)	L	Jul-Sept X
princeps	2 ft (60 cm)	SD		Mar-Apr	6 in (15 cm)	LW	Jul X
viridiflora	3 ft (90 cm)	SD		Mar-Apr	6 in (15 cm)	LW	Sept X
Gladiolus							
byzantinus	2 ft (60 cm)			Sept-Oct	6 in (15 cm)	L	June-Jul
Large-flowered hybrids	3-4 ft (90-120 cm)			Mar-May	4 in (10 cm)	B	Jul-Sept X
Butterfly hybrids	3 ft (90 cm)			Mar-May	4 in (10 cm)	B	Jul-Sept X
Gloriosa rothschildiana	6 ft (180 cm) climber			Feb-Apr	2 in (5 cm)	H 60°F (15°C)	June-Aug
Haemanthus katbreyeri	1½ ft (45 cm)			Mar	C	H 60°F (15°C)	Apr
Hedychium gardnerianum (ginger lily)	4 ft (120 cm)			Mar-Apr	C	H 45°F (7.2°C)	Jul-Sept
Hemerocallis hybrids							
'Bonanza'	2½ ft (75 cm)			Oct or Apr	C	HB	Jul-Sept X
'Chartreuse Magic'	3 ft (90 cm)			Oct or Apr	C	HB	Jul-Sept X
'Giant Moon'	2½ ft (75 cm)			Oct or Apr	C	HB	Jul-Sept X
'Nob Hill'	3 ft (90 cm)			Oct or Apr	C	HB	Jul-Sept X
'Stella d'Oro'	2 ft (60 cm)			Oct or Apr	C	HB	June-Oct X
Hepatica nobilis (syn. triloba)	4 in (10 cm)	LS		Sept-Oct	C	L	Mar-Apr
Hermodactylus tuberosus (widow iris)	10 in (25 cm)	SD		Sept-Oct	2 in (5 cm)	LW	Apr-May X
Hippeastrum	1½ ft (45 cm)			Sept-Oct	½	H 55°F (13°C)	Dec-Mar

Name			Height	Planting	Depth	Soil	Flowering
Hyacinthus (hyacinth)			8in (20cm)	Sept-Oct	6in (15cm)	L or B	Feb-Apr
Iris							
danfordiae			4in (10cm)	Sept-Oct	2in (5cm)	L	Feb-Mar
Dutch			2ft (60cm)	Sept-Oct	4in (10cm)	L or B	June X
histrioides			4in (10cm)	Sept-Oct	2in (5cm)	L or B	Jan-Mar
foetidissima (stinking gladwyn)	S-LS		1½ft (45cm)	Oct or Apr	C	L	X
reticulata			6in (15cm)	Sept-Oct	2in (5cm)	L or B	Feb-Mar
tuberosa (see *Hermodactylus tuberosus*)							
unguicularis	SFW		15in (38cm)	Sept-Oct	C	L W	Nov-Mar X
Ismene (Peruvian daffodil)							
festivalis			15in (38cm)	Mar	C	H 60°F (15°C)	June
'Sulphur Queen'			15in (38cm)	Mar	C	H 60°F (15°C)	June
Lachenalia (Cape cowslip)	SFW		8in (20cm)	Sept-Oct	S	GHFF	Mar
Lapeirousia laxa (see *Anomatheca cruenta*)							
Leucojum aestivum (snowflake)			2ft (60cm)	Sept-Oct	4in (10cm)	L	Apr
Liatris							
callilepis	SD		3ft (90cm)	Sept-Oct or Mar-Apr	1in (2.5cm)	H	Jul-Sept X
spicata	SD		2ft (60cm)	Sept-Oct or Mar-Apr	1in (2.5cm)	H	Jul-Aug X
Lilium (lily)							
auratum (golden-rayed lily of Japan)	S-LS	A	5-6ft (150-180cm)	Mar-Apr	6in (15cm)	L	Jul-Aug SCX
candidum (madonna lily)		LT	3-4ft (90-120cm)	Mar-Apr	S	L	June-Jul SCX
'Enchantment'			2-3ft (60-90cm)	Mar-Apr	6in (15cm)	L	June-Jul X
giganteum (see *Cardiocrinum giganteum*)							
longiflorum	LS	LT	2½ft (75cm)	Mar-Apr	6in (15cm)	HH	Jul-Aug SCX
martagon (Turk's cap lily)	LS	LT	4ft (120cm)	Mar-Apr	4in (10cm)	L	Jul
martagon album	S-LS	LT	4ft (120cm)	Mar-Apr	4in (10cm)	L	June-Jul
pardalinum (panther lily)	LS		4-5ft (120-150cm)	Mar-Apr	5in (13cm)	L	Jul
pumilum	SD		1½ft (45cm)	Mar-Apr	6in (15cm)	L	June
regale	S-LS	LT	3ft (90cm)	Mar-Apr	6in (15cm)	L	Jul SCX
speciosum 'Grand Commander'	S-LS	LH	4-5ft (120-150cm)	Mar-Apr	6in (15cm)	L	Aug-Sept X
s. 'Rubrum Magnificum'	S-LS	LH	5ft (150cm)	Mar-Apr	6in (15cm)	L	Aug-Sept X
s. 'Roseum'	S-LS	LH	4ft (120cm)	Mar-Apr	6in (15cm)	L	Aug-Sept X
'Stargazer'	S-LS	LH	3-4ft (90-120cm)	Mar-Apr	6in (15cm)	L	Jul X
tigrinum (tiger lily)	LS	A	4-5ft (120-150cm)	Mar-Apr	6in (15cm)	L	Aug X
tigrinum 'Splendens'	LS	A	3-4ft (90-120cm)	Mar-Apr	6in (15cm)	L	Aug X
Muscari (grape hyacinth)			5in (13cm)	Sept-Oct	3in (7.5cm)	L	Apr
Narcissus (daffodil) hybrids							
'Baby Moon'			8in (20cm)	Aug-Nov	2X	L/B	Apr-May SCX
'February Gold'			1ft (30cm)	Aug-Nov	2X	L/B	Feb-Mar
'February Silver'			1ft (30cm)	Aug-Nov	2X	L/B	Feb-Mar
'Jack Snipe'			8in (20cm)	Aug-Nov	2X	L/B	Mar
'Hawera'			7in (18cm)	Aug-Nov	2X	L/B	Apr-May
'Irene Copeland' (double)			15in (38cm)	Aug-Nov	2X	L/B	Apr
'King Alfred'			18in (45cm)	Aug-Nov	2X	L/B	Mar-Apr
'Lintie'			16in (40cm)	Aug-Nov	2X	L/B	Apr-May SC
'Love Call' (butterfly)			18in (45cm)	Aug-Nov	2X	L/B	Apr X
'Passionale' (pink)			16in (40cm)	Aug-Nov	2X	L/B	Apr

NAME and COMMON NAME	HEIGHT	SITUATION	SOIL	PLANT	DEPTH	GROW	FLOWERING
'Peeping Tom'	14 in (35 cm)			Aug–Nov	2X	L/B	Mar
'Tête-à-Tête'	6 in (15 cm)			Aug–Nov	2X	L/B	Feb–Mar
'Thalia'	16 in (40 cm)			Aug–Nov	2X	L/B	Apr–May
'Trevithian'	15 in (38 cm)			Aug–Nov	2X	L/B	Apr–May SC
'Tricolet' (butterfly)	16 in (40 cm)			Aug–Nov	2X	L/B	Apr X
'Waterperry' (pink)	10 in (25 cm)			Aug–Nov	2X	L/B	Mar–Apr
Narcissus species							
asturiensis	3 in (7.5 cm)			Aug–Nov	2X	L/B	Feb
bulbocodium	6 in (15 cm)			Aug–Nov	2X	L/B	Mar–Apr
bulbocodium romieuxii	4 in (15 cm)			Aug–Nov	2X	L/B	Oct
cyclamineus	6 in (15 cm)			Aug–Nov	2X	L/B	Feb–Mar
poeticus recurvus	15 in (38 cm)	LS		Aug–Nov	2X	L/B	May SC
pseudonarcissus	8 in (20 cm)			Aug–Nov	2X	L/B	Apr
rupicola	4 in (10 cm)			Aug–Nov	2X	L/B	Apr
triandrus albus	6 in (15 cm)			Aug–Nov	2X	L/B	Apr–May
Narcissus (specially prepared for forcing)				mid-Sept			Dec
Narcissus tazetta							
'Soleil d'Or'	14 in (35 cm)			Sept–Nov		HH 40°F (5°C)	Nov–Feb
'Paper White'	14 in (35 cm)			Sept–Nov		HH 40°F (5°C)	Nov–Feb
Nectaroscordum siculum	3 ft (90 cm)			Sept–Oct	3X	L	May–June
Nerine							
bowdenii	1½ ft (45 cm)	SFW		Aug or Apr	4 in (10 cm)	L	Sept–Oct X
crispa	1 ft (30 cm)			Aug	S	GH FF	Oct–Nov
Hybrids	2 ft (60 cm)			Aug	S	GH FF	Sept–Nov
sarniensis (Guernsey lily)	2 ft (60 cm)			Aug	S	GH FF	Sept–Nov
Oxalis							
adenophylla	4 in (10 cm)	SD		Sept or Mar	2 in (5 cm)	L	May–June
versicolor	6 in (15 cm)			Sept	C	GH FF	Nov–Mar
Pleione (windowsill orchid)	4 in (10 cm)			Jan–Feb	½	GH FF	Apr–May
Polianthes tuberosa (tuberose) 'The Pearl'	2–3 ft (60–90 cm)			Feb–Mar	S	GH FF	Aug–Sept SC
Rhodohypoxis baurii hybrids	4 in (10 cm)			Feb–Mar	C	GH FF	May–Sept
Sauromatum venosum	1½ ft (45 cm)			Feb–Mar	C	H/GH FF	May
Schizostylis							
coccinea (Kaffir lilly)	2 ft (60 cm)		M	Sept–Oct or Apr	C	HB	Sept–Nov X
S.c. 'Mrs Hegarty'	2 ft (60 cm)		M	Sept–Oct or Apr	C	HB	Sept–Nov X
Sisyrinchium							
bellum	4 in (10 cm)			Sept–Oct or Apr	C	HB	May–Aug
brachypus	4 in (10 cm)			Sept–Oct or Apr	C	HB	June–Sept
striatum	18 in (45 cm)			Sept–Oct or Apr	C	HB	June–Jul

	Height	Code	Planting time	Depth	Temp	Flowering
Sternbergia						
lutea	4 in (10 cm)		Aug–Sept	5 in (13 cm)	L	Sept–Oct
clusiana	6 in (15 cm)		Aug–Sept	5 in (13 cm)	L	Sept–Nov
Tigridia pavonia	2 ft (60 cm)		Apr–May	4 in (10 cm)	HH	Jul–Sep
Tricyrtis (toad lily)						
hirta	1½ ft (45 cm)	LS	Sept–Oct or Apr	C	HB	Aug–Oct
formosana stolonifera	2 ft (60 cm)	LS	Sept–Oct or Apr	C	HB	Aug–Oct
Tulipa (tulip)						
Parrot tulips						
'Apricot Parrot'	1½ ft (45 cm)		Nov	6 in (15 cm)	L/B	May X
'Black Parrot'	2 ft (60 cm)		Nov	6 in (15 cm)	L/B	May X
Lily-flowered tulips						
'White Triumphator'	2 ft (60 cm)		Nov	6 in (15 cm)	L/B	May X
Cottage tulips – Viridiflora						
'Angel'	14 in (35 cm)		Nov	6 in (15 cm)	L/B	May X
'Florosa'	14 in (35 cm)		Nov	6 in (15 cm)	L/B	May X
Other tulip hybrids						
'Queen of the Night'	2 ft (60 cm)		Nov	6 in (15 cm)	L/B	May X
'Apeldoorn'	2 ft (60 cm)		Nov	6 in (15 cm)	L/B	Apr–May X
Water-lily tulips						
Kaufmanniana hybrids	6–8 in (15–20 cm)		Nov	6 in (15 cm)	L/B	Mar
'Ancilla'	6 in (15 cm)		Nov	6 in (15 cm)	L/B	Mar
Fosteriana hybrids	6–8 in (15–20 cm)		Nov	6 in (15 cm)	L/B	Mar
Tulip species						
acuminata (horned tulip)	18 in (45 cm)	SD	Nov	6 in (15 cm)	B	May
clusiana (lady tulip)	10 in (25 cm)	SD	Nov	6 in (15 cm)	B	Apr
orphanidea	8 in (20 cm)	SD	Nov	6 in (15 cm)	B	Apr
pulchella	5 in (13 cm)	SD	Nov	6 in (15 cm)	B	Mar
pulchella violacea	5 in (13 cm)	SD	Nov	6 in (15 cm)	B	Feb
turkestanica	9 in (23 cm)	SD	Nov	6 in (15 cm)	B	Mar
Vallota speciosa (Scarborough lily)	1 ft (30 cm)		Mar–Apr	S	H	Sept–Oct
Veltheimia viridiflora	1½ ft (45 cm)		Sept	S	H/GH 40°F (5°C)	Dec–Jan
Zantedeschia						
aethiopica (arum lily)	2–3 ft (60–90 cm)		Mar	C	GH	Apr–June
elliottiana	1½ ft (45 cm)		Mar	C	H 60°F (15°C)	May–June
rehmannii	1 ft (30 cm)		Mar	C	H 60°F (15°C)	May–June
Zephyranthes (zephyr lily)						
candida	6 in (15 cm)	SD	Mar–Apr	1 in (2.5 cm)	L	Sept–Oct
robusta	6 in (15 cm)	SD	Mar–Apr	1 in (2.5 cm)	HH	Sept

USEFUL REFERENCE BOOKS

Collins Guide to Bulbs Patrick M. Synge, Collins, 1961

The Bulb Book Martyn Rix and Roger Phillips, Pan Books, 1981

The Smaller Bulbs Brian Matthew, Batsford, 1987

Dwarf Bulbs Brian Matthew, Batsford, 1973

Royal Horticultural Society *Gardeners' Encyclopaedia of Plants and Flowers* ed. Chris Brickell, Dorling Kindersley, 1989

The Plant Finder published annually by Headmain Ltd for the Hardy Plant Society. Contains information on where to put particular plants, including bulbs

MAIL ORDER NURSERIES SUPPLYING PLANTS MENTIONED IN THIS BOOK

Some nurseries will require a s.a.e. and/or payment for catalogues. It may be advisable to check before applying.

LARGE FIRMS SUPPLYING GENERAL ILLUSTRATED CATALOGUES

Walter Blom & Son Ltd
Coombelands Nurseries
Leavesden
Watford
Herts WD2 7BH
0923 672071

P. de Jager & Sons Ltd
The Nurseries
Marden
Kent TN12 9BP
0622 831235

Bressingham Gardens
Diss
Norfolk IP22 2AB
0379 88464

(herbaceous, e.g. tricyrtis, hemerocallis, crocosmia)

Van Tubergen UK Ltd
Bressingham
Diss
Norfolk IP22 2AP
0379 888282

SMALL FIRMS SPECIALISING IN UNUSUAL BULBS

Jacques Armand
Clamp Hill
Stanmore
Middx HA7 3JS
081 954 8138

Paul Christian
PO Box 468
Wrexham
Clwyd LL13 9XR
0978 366399

Avon Bulbs
Burnt House Farm
Mid Lambrook
South Petherton
Somerset TA13 5HE
0460 42177

Rupert Bowlby
Gatton
Reigate
Surrey RH2 0TA
07374 2221

Potterton & Martin
The Cottage Nursery
Moortown Road
Nettleton
Nr Caister
Lincs LN7 6HX
0472 851792

(dwarf bulbs)

Broadleigh Gardens
1 Bishops Hull
Taunton
Somerset
0823 286231

(dwarf bulbs)

Cambridge Bulbs
40 Whittlesford Road
Newton
Cambs CB2 5PH
0223 871760

(dwarf bulbs)

John Chambers
15 Westleigh Road
Barton Seagrave
Kettering
Northants NN15 5AJ
0933 652562

(wild flower bulbs)

INDEX

Photographs in *italics*.

Acidanthera murielae 63, 68, 77, 102
African lily see Agapanthus
Agapanthus 72, 83, *86*, 89, 93, *95*, 102
Agapanthus africanus
  'Bressingham Blue' 89, 93, *95*, 102
  'Blue Giant' 89, 93, *95*, 102
Agapanthus patens 102
Allium 63–4, *66*, 72–3, *77*, 102
Allium albopilosum 64, 77, 102
Allium bulgaricum see *Nectaroscordum siculum*
Allium cernum 73, 102
Allium giganteum 64, 77, 102
Allium karataviense 64, 102
Allium oreophilum 72, 102
Allium pulchellum 73, 102
Allium sphaerocephalum 64, *66*, 77, 102
Alstroemeria 77, 102
  'Ligtu Hybrids' 77, 102
Alstroemeria aurantiaca 77, 102
Alstroemeria pulchella 77, 102
Amaryllis belladonna 88, 89, *90*, 103
Anemone 14, 36–7, *38*, 49, 103
Anemone blanda 38, 36–7, 103
Anemone coronia 14, 103
  'De Caen' 14, 103
  'St Brigid' 103
Anemone nemorosa 49, 103
Angel's fishing rod see *Dierama*
Anomatheca cruenta 73, 103, 105
Arum italicum 'Pictum' *36*, 49, 103
Arum lily see *Zantedeschia aethiopica* 107
Autumn-flowering bulbs 83–101

Begonias 11, 20, *23*, 69, 103
  pendulous 103
  tuberous 11, 20, *23*, 69, 103
Bluebell see *Endymion nonscriptus*

Border planting of bulbs 16–17, 33–40, 64–9, 84–9, *95*
Bulbs
  autumn- and winter-flowering 83–101
  in borders 16–17, 33–40, 64–9, 84–9, *95*
  in containers 32, 40, 44, 53, 56–7, 69–72, 84, *86*, 89–91, 96
  for cut flowers 28–9, *51*, 52–3, *70*, 76–9, *90*, 93, *94*
  definition of 8–10
  feeding of 16, 20–1, 24, 29, 60, 80, 97
  as houseplants 24–5, 27, 53–6, 79–81, 84–5, *86*, *91*, 93–7, 99
  naturalising of 11, *15*, 16–20, 44, 49–52, *67*, 76, *87*, *91*, 92
  in raised beds 21–4, 44–8, 92
  in rockeries 21–4, 43–8, *55*, 72–5, *91*, 92
  in sink gardens, 21–4, 44–8, *55*, 72–5, 92
  spring-flowering 31–61
  summer-flowering 63–81
  under glass 25–7, 56–61, *91*, 97–101, 99
  watering of 25, 28, 60, 80
  in woodland gardens *34*, 48–9, 75–6, 78

Camassia esculenta 76, 103
Canna 20, 103
Cape cowslip see *Lachenalia*
Cardiocrinum giganteum 20, 76, 78, 103, 105
Chinese sacred lily see *Narcissus tazetta*
Clivia miniata 54, *54*, 85, 103
Colchicum 85–9, 91–2, 96–7, 100, 103
Colchicum aggripinum 92, 103
Colchicum autumnale 87
Colchicum speciosum

'Lilac Wonder' 88, 96, 103
'Water Lily' 88, *91*, 92, 96, 103
Compost 16, 20–2, 24, 27–8, 57, 59, 80
  John Innes potting compost No. 2 21, 59
Container-grown bulbs 32, 40, 44, 53, 56–7, 69–72, 84, *86*, 89–91, 96
Convallaria majalis 27, 37, 52–4, 103
Crocosmia 65–6, *70*, 103
Crocus 27, 31–2, 41, *51*, 83, 85–6, 88, 92, *97*, 100, 103
  autumn-flowering 83, 85, 89, 92, 97, 103
  spring-flowering 86, 103
Crocus sativa 92, 103
Crocus speciosa 88, *90*, 103
Crown imperial see *Fritillaria imperialis*
Cut flowers from bulbs 28–9, *51*, 52–3, *70*, 76–9, *90*, 93, *94*
Cyclamen 9, 12, 21, 49, 56–7, 88, 92, *94*, 99, 100–1, 103
Cyclamen africanum 100, 103
Cyclamen coum 49, 56, 103
  'Pewter' 100, 103
Cyclamen cyprium 101, 103
Cyclamen graecum 101, 103
Cyclamen hederifolium 92, *94*
Cyclamen libanoticum 57, 101
Cyclamen neapolitanum 88, 103
Cyclamen persicum 57, 99, 101, 103
Cyclamen purpurascens 88, 92, 103
Cyclamen trochopteranthum 57, 103

Daffodil 11, 17, *18*, 37, 41–4, 52, 96
  butterfly see *Narcissus* hybrids 'Love Call' and 'Tricolet'
  double see *Narcissus* hybrid 'Irene Copeland'
  pink see *Narcissus* hybrids 'Passionale' and 'Waterperry'
  see also *Narcissus* hybrids

Dierama 63, 74–5, *79*, 103
Dierama pendulum 75, 103
Dierama pulcherrimum 75, 103
Dog's tooth violet see *Erythronium dens-canis*
Dormancy 11–12, 20, 24, 45

Endymion nonscriptus 17, 19, 48, 103
Eranthis hyemalis 31, 37, 49, 103
Eremurus 68, *71*, 104
  'Shelford Hybrids' 104
Eremurus elwessii 71
Eremurus robustus 68, 104
Erythronium 49, 104
Erythronium dens-canis 49, 104
Erythronium tuolumnense 49, 104
Eucharis grandiflora 79, 104
Eucomis 72, 74, *74*, 104
Eucomis bicolor 74, 104

Feeding of bulbs 16, 20, 21, 24, 29, 60, 80, 97
Flower of the west wind see *Zephyranthes*
Foxtail lily see *Eremurus*
Freesias 59, 104
Fritillaria acmopetala 48, 104
Fritillaria imperialis 16, 21, 40, 104
Fritillaria lactifolia nobilis 59
Fritillaria meleagris *47*, 49, 50, 104
  'Aphrodite' 49, 104
Fritillaria michailovskii 48, 104
Fritillaria persica 40, *42*, 104

Galanthus 12, *19*, 27, 31, 36–7, 41, 49, 51, 53, 100, 104
Galanthus nivalis 104
Galanthus reginae-olgae 100, 104
Galtonia 69, 77, 104
Galtonia candicans 69, 104
Galtonia princeps 69, 104
Galtonia viridiflora 69, 104
Garden centres 11, 13, 96
Giant Himalayan lily see *Cardiocrinum giganteum*
Ginger lily see *Hedychium gardnerianum*
Gladioli 11, 28, 68, *70*, 76, 104
  butterfly 104
  large-flowered 104
Gladiolus byzantinus 68, 104
Gloriosa rothschildiana 79, 80, 104

Golden-rayed lily of Japan see *Lilium auratum*
Grape hyacinth see *Muscari*
Guernsey lily see *Nerine bowdenii sarniendis*

Haemanthus 77, 80, 104
Haemanthus kalbreyeri 80, 104
Hedychium 80, 104
Hedychium gardnerianum 80, 104
Hemerocallis hybrids 65–6, 83, 93, 104
  'Bonanza' 93, 104
  'Chartreuse Magic' 93, 104
  'Giant Moon' 93, 104
  'Nob Hill' 93, 104
  'Stella d'Oro' 93, 104
Hepatica nobilis 45, 104
Hermodactylus tuberosus 104
Himalayan lily see *Cardiocrinum giganteum*
Hippeastrum 25, 54, 56, 89, 95, 104
Horned tulip see *Tulipa acuminata*
Houseplants 24–5, 27, 53–6, 79–81, 84–6, *91*, 93–7, 99
Hyacinth 20, *27*, 33, 41, *42*, 53, 96–7, 105

Iris 23, 45, 47, 52, 57, *58*, 93, *94*, 105
  Dutch 52, 105
Iris danfordiae 57, 105
Iris foetidissima (gladwyn) 93, 105
  'Bressingham Comet' 93
  'Little Maid' 93
  'Percy's Pride' 93
Iris histrioides 57, 105
Iris reticulata 23, 45, 57, *58*, 105
Iris tuberosa see *Hermodactylus tuberosus*
Iris unguicularis 36, 93, *94*, 105
  'Mary Barnard' 94
Ismene 80, 105
  'Sulphur Queen' 80, 105
Ismene festivalis 80, 105

Kaffir lily
  indoor see *Clivia miniata*
  outdoor see *Schizostylis coccinea*

Lachenalia 54–6, 105
Lady tulip see *Tulipa clusiana*

Lapeirousia cruenta see *Anomatheca cruenta*
Lapeirousia laxa see *Anomatheca cruenta*
Leucojum aestivum 36, 105
Liatris 63, 69, 93, *95*, 105
Liatris callilepis 93, 105
Liatris spicata 105
Lilies 11, *14*, 17, 22, 48, 63–5, 67, 72, 74, 75–7, *79*, 84–5, *86*, 105
Lilium auratum 65, 105
Lilium candidum 65, 105
Lilium giganteum see *Cardiocrinum giganteum*
Lilium longiflorum 77, 105
Lilium martagon 65, *67*, 76, 105
  album 105
Lilium pardalinum 76, 105
Lilium pumilum 72, 105
Lilium regale 65, 105
Lilium speciosum
  'Black Magic' 22
  'Enchantment' 77, 105
  'Grand Commander' 84, 105
  'Roseum' 84, 105
  'Rubrum Magnificum' 84, *86*, 105
  'Stargazer' 77, 105
Lilium tigrinum 65, 72, *74*, 105
  splendens 76, 105
Lily of the valley see *Convallaria majalis*

Madonna lily see *Lilium candidum*
Montbretia see *Crocosmia*
Muscari 36, 41, *43*, 47, 51, 105

Narcissus asturiensis 44, 106
Narcissus bulbocodium 100, 106
  romieuxii 100, 106
Narcissus cyclamineus 45, 57, 106
Narcissus hybrids 17, *18*, 20, 21, 31, 33, 34, 36, 43, 44, 53, 105–6
  'Baby Moon' 43, 105
  'February Gold' 17, *18*, 33, *34*, 43, 105
  'February Silver' 43, 105
  'Jack Snipe' 43, 105
  'Hawera' 43, 105
  'Irene Copeland' 33, 105
  'King Alfred' 105
  'Lintie' 43, 105
  'Love Call' 33, 105

'Passionale' 36, 105
'Peeping Tom' 43, 106
'Tête-à-Tête' 33, 43, 106
'Thalia' 43, 106
'Trevithian' 43, 106
'Tricolet' 33, 106
'Waterperry' 36, 106
Narcissus jonquilla 57
Narcissus poeticus
   'Flore Pleno' 51
   recurvus 51, 106
Narcissus pseudonarcissus 49, 106
Narcissus rupicola 57, 106
Narcissus triandrus albus 106
Narcissus tazetta 24, 97, 100, 106
   'Paper White' 24, 97
   'Soleil d'Or' 24, 97, 106
Naturalising of bulbs 11, 15, 16-21, 44, 49-52, 67, 76, 87, 91, 92
Nectaroscordum siculum 64, 106
Nerine bowdenii 88, 99, 100, 106
   crispa 100, 106
   hybrids 88, 99, 100, 106
   sarniendis 100, 106

Ornamental onion see Allium
Oxalis adenophylla 55, 57, 106
Oxalis versicolor 57, 106

Panther lily see Lilium paradalinum
Peruvian daffodil see Ismene
Peruvian lily see Alstroemeria
Pineapple flower see Eucomis bicolor
Pleione orchids 57, 58, 106
Polianthes tuberosa 81, 106
   'The Pearl' 81, 106

Quamash see Camassia esculenta

Raised beds 21-4, 44-8, 92
Rhodohypoxis baurii hybrids 73, 75, 106
Rockeries 21-4, 43-8, 55, 72-5, 91, 92
Royal Horticultural Society Gardens at Wisley 57, 79

Saffron crocus see Crocus sativus
Sauromatum venosum 56, 106
Scarborough lily see Vallota speciosa 107
Schizostylis 83, 85, 87, 89, 93, 96-7, 106
Schizostylis coccinea 83, 85, 106
   'Mrs Hegarty' 85, 87, 106
Sink gardens 21-4, 44-8, 55, 72-5, 92
Sisyrinchium 73, 106
Sisyrinchium bellum 73, 106
Sisyrinchium brachypus 73, 106
Sisyrinchium striatum 73, 75, 106
Snake's head fritillary see Fritillaria meleagris
Snowdrop see Galanthus
Snowflake see Leucojum aestivum
Soil 12-13, 16, 20-2, 78, 89
   acidity of 13, 22, 78
   type of 13, 16, 20, 21, 22, 89
Spring-flowering bulbs 31-61
Sternbergia 86, 89, 92, 94, 106
Sternbergia clausia 92, 106
Sternbergia lutea 86, 88, 94
Stinking gladwyn see Iris foetidissima
Summer-flowering bulbs 63-81
Summer hyacinth see Galtonia

Tiger lily see Lilium tigrinum
Tigridia 20, 63, 68, 71, 107
Tigridia pavonia 68, 107
Toad lilies see Tricyrtis hirta
Tricyrtis 84-5, 91
Tricyrtis hirta 84-5, 107
Tricyrtis formosana stolonifera 84, 91, 107
Tuberose see Polianthes tuberosa
Tulipa acuminata 45, 107
Tulipa clusiana 45, 107
Tulipa fosteriana hybrids 41, 44, 107
Tulipa kaufmanniana hybrids 41, 42, 44, 107
Tulipa orphanidea 45, 57, 107
Tulipa pulchella 45, 107

violacea 45, 107
Tulipa turkestanica 45, 107
Tulips 17, 20, 28, 34, 37, 39, 40-5, 48, 51-3, 57, 96, 107
   cottage 37, 52, 107
      'Angel' 37, 107
      'Florosa' 37, 107
      'Greenland' 39
   hybrid 37, 107
      'Apeldoorn' 107
      'Queen of the Night' 40, 107
   lily-flowered 37, 107
      'White Triumphator' 37, 107
   parrot 37, 39, 107
      'Apricot Parrot' 37, 39
      'Black Parrot' 40, 107
   water-lily 42, 51, 107
      'Ancilla' 107
   see also Tulipa species
Turk's cap lily see Lilium martagon

Vallota speciosa 24, 95, 100, 107
Veltheimia 95, 100, 107
Veltheimia viridiflora 107
   see also Tulips, cottage
Voodoo lily see Sauromatum venosum

Watering of bulbs 25, 28, 60, 80
Widow iris see Hermodactylus tuberosus
Window sill orchid see Pleione
Winter aconite see Eranthis hyemalis
Wood anemone see Anemone nemorosa
Wood sorrel 17, 49
Woodland gardens 34, 48-9, 75-6, 78

Zantedeschia 81, 89, 107
Zantedeschia aethiopica 81, 107
Zantedeschia elliottiana 81, 107
Zantedeschia rehmannii 89, 107
Zephyr lily see Zephyranthes
Zephyranthes 89, 91, 92, 107
Zephyranthes candida 89, 91, 107
Zephyranthes robusta 89, 91, 92, 107